Pennsylvania State Parks Bucket Journal

This Journal Belongs to:

....

....

Packing List

- ☐ CAMERA
- ☐ PARK MAP
- ☐ TRASH BAG
- ☐ WARM SWEATER
- ☐ BINOCULARS
- ☐ MAGNIFYING GLASS
- ☐ WATER BOTTLE
- ☐ SNACKS
- ☐ SWIMSUIT AND TOWEL
- ☐ FIRST AID KIT AND SNAKE BITE KIT
- ☐ HAT
- ☐ SUNBLOCK
- ☐ PEN AND PENCIL
- ☐ BACKPACK
- ☐ FIELD GUIDE
- ☐ D'ONT FORGET TO PACK THIS BOOK!

Anything Else?

List of Pennsylvania State Parks

PARK NAME	COUNTY OR COUNTIES	VISITED	DATE
Allegheny Islands State Park	Allegheny		
Archbald Pothole State Park	Lackawanna		
Bald Eagle State Park	Centre		
Beltzville State Park	Carbon		
Bendigo State Park	Elk		
Benjamin Rush State Park	Philadelphia		
Big Pocono State Park	Monroe		
Big Spring State Forest Picnic Area	Perry		
Black Moshannon State Park	Centre		
Blue Knob State Park	Bedford		
Boyd Big Tree Preserve Conservation Area	Dauphin		
Buchanan's Birthplace State Park	Franklin		
Bucktail State Park Natural Area	Cameron and Clinton		
Caledonia State Park	Adams and Franklin		
Canoe Creek State Park	Blair		
Chapman State Park	Warren		
Cherry Springs State Park	Potter		
Clear Creek State Park	Jefferson		
Codorus State Park	York		
Colonel Denning State Park	Cumberland		
Colton Point State Park	Tioga		
Cook Forest State Park	Clarion, Forest, and Jefferson		
Cowans Gap State Park	Franklin and Fulton		
Delaware Canal State Park	Bucks and Northampton		
Denton Hill State Park	Potter		
Elk State Park	Elk and McKean		

PARK NAME	COUNTY OR COUNTIES	VISITED	DATE
Erie Bluffs State Park	Erie		
Evansburg State Park	Montgomery		
Fort Washington State Park	Montgomery		
Fowlers Hollow State Park	Perry		
Frances Slocum State Park	Luzerne		
French Creek State Park	Berks and Chester		
Gifford Pinchot State Park	York		
Gouldsboro State Park	Monroe and Wayne		
Greenwood Furnace State Park	Huntingdon		
Hickory Run State Park	Carbon		
Hillman State Park	Washington		
Hills Creek State Park	Tioga		
Hyner Run State Park	Clinton		
Hyner View State Park	Clinton		
Jacobsburg Environmental Education Center	Northampton		
Jennings Environmental Education Center	Butler		
Joseph E. Ibberson Conservation Area	Dauphin		
Kettle Creek State Park	Clinton		
Keystone State Park	Westmoreland		
Kings Gap Environmental Education and Training Center	Cumberland		
Kinzua Bridge State Park	McKean		
Kooser State Park	Somerset		
Lackawanna State Park	Lackawanna		
Laurel Hill State Park	Somerset		
Laurel Mountain State Park	Somerset and Westmoreland		
Laurel Ridge State Park	Cambria, Fayette, Somerset and Westmoreland		
Laurel Summit State Park	Westmoreland		
Lehigh Gorge State Park	Carbon and Luzerne		
Leonard Harrison State Park	Tioga		

PARK NAME	COUNTY OR COUNTIES	VISITED	DATE
Linn Run State Park	Westmoreland		
Little Buffalo State Park	Perry		
Little Pine State Park	Lycoming		
Locust Lake State Park	Schuylkill		
Lyman Run State Park	Potter		
Marsh Creek State Park	Chester		
Maurice K. Goddard State Park	Mercer		
McCalls Dam State Park	Centre		
McConnells Mill State Park	Lawrence		
Memorial Lake State Park	Lebanon		
Milton State Park	Northumberland		
Mont Alto State Park	Franklin		
Moraine State Park	Butler		
Mt. Pisgah State Park	Bradford		
Nescopeck State Park	Luzerne		
Neshaminy State Park	Bucks		
Nockamixon State Park	Bucks		
Nolde Forest Environmental Education Center	Berks		
Norristown Farm Park	Montgomery		
Ohiopyle State Park	Fayette		
Oil Creek State Park	Venango		
Ole Bull State Park	Potter		
Parker Dam State Park	Clearfield		
Patterson State Park	Potter		
Penn-Roosevelt State Park	Centre		
Pine Grove Furnace State Park	Cumberland		
Poe Paddy State Park	Centre		
Poe Valley State Park	Centre		
Point State Park	Allegheny		

PARK NAME	COUNTY OR COUNTIES	VISITED	DATE
Presque Isle State Park	Erie		
Prince Gallitzin State Park	Cambria		
Promised Land State Park	Pike		
Prompton State Park	Wayne		
Prouty Place State Park	Potter		
Pymatuning State Park	Crawford		
Raccoon Creek State Park	Beaver		
Ralph Stover State Park	Bucks		
Ravensburg State Park	Clinton		
Reeds Gap State Park	Mifflin		
R. B. Winter State Park	Union		
Ricketts Glen State Park	Columbia, Luzerne, and Sullivan		
Ridley Creek State Park	Delaware		
Ryerson Station State Park	Greene		
Salt Springs State Park	Susquehanna		
Samuel S. Lewis State Park	York		
Sand Bridge State Park	Union		
Shawnee State Park	Bedford		
Shikellamy State Park	Northumberland and Union		
Simon B. Elliott State Park	Clearfield		
Sinnemahoning State Park	Cameron and Potter		
Sizerville State Park	Cameron and Potter		
Susquehanna State Park	Lycoming		
Susquehannock State Park	Lancaster		
Swatara State Park	Lebanon and Schuylkill		
Tobyhanna State Park	Monroe and Wayne		
Trough Creek State Park	Huntingdon		
Tuscarora State Park	Schuylkill		
Tyler State Park	Bucks		

PARK NAME	COUNTY OR COUNTIES	VISITED	DATE
Upper Pine Bottom State Park	Lycoming		
Varden Conservation Area	Wayne		
Warriors Path State Park	Bedford		
Washington Crossing Historic Park	Bucks		
Whipple Dam State Park	Huntingdon		
White Clay Creek Preserve	Chester		
Worlds End State Park	Sullivan		
Yellow Creek State Park	Indiana		

Allegheny Islands State Park

DATE(S) VISITED:..

❏ SPRING   ❏ SUMMER   ❏ FALL   ❏ WINTER

WEATHER						TEMP:
☀	❄☁	☁	☁🌧	☁🌧	☁🌨	
❏	❏	❏	❏	❏	❏	

Check In:............................. Check Out:..............................

Lodging:................................. Park hours:........................

Who I Went With:...

Fee(s):.. Will I Return?   YES / NO

Rating ★ ★ ★ ★ ★

ABOUT THIS STATE PARK

Accessible only by boat, the 50-acre Allegheny Islands State Park consists of two alluvial islands and seven shoals in the Allegheny River. The park is heavily covered in vegetation and remains undeveloped. Some of the few islands left in a natural state, the islands are homes to many animals and plants and frequently flood.
There are no developed trails, however, several footpaths exist.

Activities

❏ ATV/OHV   ❏ Horseback Riding   ❏ Fishing   ❏ Wildlife
❏ Berry Picking   ❏ Kayaking   ❏ Hiking   ❏ Bird Viewing
❏ Biking   ❏ Photography   ❏ Hunting   ❏ Snowmobiling
❏ Boating   ❏ Skiing   ❏ Snowshoeing   ❏ ....
❏ Canoeing   ❏ Skijoring   ❏ Swimming   ❏ ....

Facilities

❏ ADA   ❏ Visitor Center   ❏ Museum   ❏ ....
❏ Gift Shop   ❏ Picnic Sites   ❏ Restrooms   ❏ ....

Notes

....
....
....
....

Passport Stamps

Archbald Pothole State Park

Lackawanna

DATE(S) VISITED:..

❑ SPRING   ❑ SUMMER   ❑ FALL   ❑ WINTER

WEATHER	TEMP:

☀ ❑   ☀☁ ❑   ☁ ❑   🌧 ❑   🌧 ❑   🌨 ❑

Check In:............................. Check Out:..............................

Lodging:................................. Park hours:.........................

Who I Went With:..

Fee(s):.. Will I Return?   YES / NO

Rating   ⭐ ⭐ ⭐ ⭐ ⭐

ABOUT THIS STATE PARK

Archbald Pothole State Park is a 150-acre park in northeastern Pennsylvania. The park is named for Archbald Pothole, a geologic feature that formed during the Wisconsin Glacial Period, around 15,000 years ago. The pothole is 38 feet deep and has an elliptical shape. The diameter of the pothole decreases downward. The largest diameter is 42 feet by 24 feet. At the bottom it is 17 feet by 14 feet. The pothole has a volume of about 18,600 cubic feet.

Activities

❑ ATV/OHV	❑ Horseback Riding	❑ Fishing	❑ Wildlife
❑ Berry Picking	❑ Kayaking	❑ Hiking	❑ Bird Viewing
❑ Biking	❑ Photography	❑ Hunting	❑ Snowmobiling
❑ Boating	❑ Skiing	❑ Snowshoeing	❑ ....
❑ Canoeing	❑ Skijoring	❑ Swimming	❑ ....

Facilities

❑ ADA	❑ Visitor Center	❑ Museum	❑ ....
❑ Gift Shop	❑ Picnic Sites	❑ Restrooms	❑ ....

Notes

....
....
....
....

Passport Stamps

Bald Eagle State Park

Centre

DATE(S) VISITED:..

❏ SPRING ❏ SUMMER ❏ FALL ❏ WINTER

WEATHER			TEMP:		
❏	❏	❏	❏	❏	❏

Check In:............................. Check Out:...............................

Lodging:.................................. Park hours:........................

Who I Went With:...

Fee(s):.. Will I Return? YES / NO

Rating ★ ★ ★ ★ ★

Activities

❏ ATV/OHV	❏ Horseback Riding	❏ Fishing	❏ Wildlife
❏ Berry Picking	❏ Kayaking	❏ Hiking	❏ Bird Viewing
❏ Biking	❏ Photography	❏ Hunting	❏ Snowmobiling
❏ Boating	❏ Skiing	❏ Snowshoeing	❏ ....
❏ Canoeing	❏ Skijoring	❏ Swimming	❏ ....

Facilities

❏ ADA	❏ Visitor Center	❏ Museum	❏ ....
❏ Gift Shop	❏ Picnic Sites	❏ Restrooms	❏ ....

Notes

....
....
....
....

Passport Stamps

Beltzville State Park

DATE(S) VISITED:..

❑ SPRING   ❑ SUMMER   ❑ FALL   ❑ WINTER

WEATHER	TEMP:

❑ ❑ ❑ ❑ ❑ ❑

ABOUT THIS STATE PARK

Check In:................................ Check Out:...............................

Lodging:.................................... Park hours:.........................

Who I Went With:...

Fee(s):.. Will I Return?   YES / NO

The 3,002-acre Beltzville State Park is in the southern foothills of the Poconos. Pohopoco Creek, an excellent trout stream, feeds the 949-acre Beltzville Lake, which is a rest stop for migrating waterfowl and is a destination for boaters and anglers. The sand beach and picnic pavilions are very popular.

Rating ★ ★ ★ ★ ★

Activities

❑ ATV/OHV	❑ Horseback Riding	❑ Fishing	❑ Wildlife
❑ Berry Picking	❑ Kayaking	❑ Hiking	❑ Bird Viewing
❑ Biking	❑ Photography	❑ Hunting	❑ Snowmobiling
❑ Boating	❑ Skiing	❑ Snowshoeing	❑ ....
❑ Canoeing	❑ Skijoring	❑ Swimming	❑ ....

Facilities

❑ ADA	❑ Visitor Center	❑ Museum	❑ ....
❑ Gift Shop	❑ Picnic Sites	❑ Restrooms	❑ ....

Notes

....
....
....
....

Passport Stamps

Bendigo State Park

Elk

DATE(S) VISITED:...

☐ SPRING ☐ SUMMER ☐ FALL ☐ WINTER

WEATHER		TEMP:

☀ ☐ 🌤 ☐ ☁ ☐ 🌧 ☐ ⛈ ☐ 🌨 ☐

Check In:............................ Check Out:.............................

Lodging:................................. Park hours:.......................

Who I Went With:...

Fee(s):.. Will I Return? YES / NO

Rating ⭐⭐⭐⭐⭐

Activities

☐ ATV/OHV
☐ Berry Picking
☐ Biking
☐ Boating
☐ Canoeing
☐ Horseback Riding
☐ Kayaking
☐ Photography
☐ Skiing
☐ Skijoring
☐ Fishing
☐ Hiking
☐ Hunting
☐ Snowshoeing
☐ Swimming
☐ Wildlife
☐ Bird Viewing
☐ Snowmobiling
☐ ....
☐ ....

Facilities

☐ ADA
☐ Gift Shop
☐ Visitor Center
☐ Picnic Sites
☐ Museum
☐ Restrooms
☐ ....
☐ ....

Notes

....
....
....
....

Passport Stamps

Benjamin Rush State Park   Philadelphia

DATE(S) VISITED:..

☐ SPRING   ☐ SUMMER   ☐ FALL   ☐ WINTER

WEATHER			TEMP:		
☀	❄	☁	🌧	⛈	🌨
☐	☐	☐	☐	☐	☐

Check In:............................. Check Out:.............................

Lodging:................................. Park hours:.......................

Who I Went With:..

Fee(s):.. Will I Return?   YES / NO

Rating ⭐ ⭐ ⭐ ⭐ ⭐

Activities

☐ ATV/OHV	☐ Horseback Riding	☐ Fishing	☐ Wildlife
☐ Berry Picking	☐ Kayaking	☐ Hiking	☐ Bird Viewing
☐ Biking	☐ Photography	☐ Hunting	☐ Snowmobiling
☐ Boating	☐ Skiing	☐ Snowshoeing	☐ ....
☐ Canoeing	☐ Skijoring	☐ Swimming	☐ ....

Facilities

☐ ADA	☐ Visitor Center	☐ Museum	☐ ....
☐ Gift Shop	☐ Picnic Sites	☐ Restrooms	☐ ....

Notes

....
....
....
....

Passport Stamps

Big Pocono State Park

DATE(S) VISITED:..

❑ SPRING ❑ SUMMER ❑ FALL ❑ WINTER

WEATHER	TEMP:

❑   ❑   ❑   ❑   ❑   ❑

Check In:............................. Check Out:...............................

Lodging:................................. Park hours:........................

Who I Went With:..

Fee(s):... Will I Return? YES / NO

Rating ⭐ ⭐ ⭐ ⭐ ⭐

ABOUT THIS STATE PARK

Big Pocono State Park is in Monroe County in northeastern Pennsylvania. The park consists of 1,306 acres of rugged terrain on the summit and slopes of Camelback Mountain and features scenic views of three states.visitors can enjoy a magnificent view of a vast portion of eastern Pennsylvania and portions of New Jersey and New York.

Activities

❑ ATV/OHV	❑ Horseback Riding	❑ Fishing	❑ Wildlife
❑ Berry Picking	❑ Kayaking	❑ Hiking	❑ Bird Viewing
❑ Biking	❑ Photography	❑ Hunting	❑ Snowmobiling
❑ Boating	❑ Skiing	❑ Snowshoeing	❑ ....
❑ Canoeing	❑ Skijoring	❑ Swimming	❑ ....

Facilities

❑ ADA	❑ Visitor Center	❑ Museum	❑ ....
❑ Gift Shop	❑ Picnic Sites	❑ Restrooms	❑ ....

Notes

....
....
....
....

Passport Stamps

Big Spring State Forest Picnic Area

Perry

DATE(S) VISITED:..

❑ SPRING　　❑ SUMMER　　❑ FALL　　❑ WINTER

WEATHER	TEMP:
☀ ❑　✴☁ ❑　☁ ❑　🌧 ❑　⛈ ❑　🌨 ❑	

Check In:............................. Check Out:............................

Lodging:.................................. Park hours:.......................

Who I Went With:..

Fee(s):.. Will I Return?　YES / NO

Rating　⭐ ⭐ ⭐ ⭐ ⭐

ABOUT THIS STATE PARK

Tucked in the side of Conococheague Mountain, Big Spring State Park is a quaint picnic and hiking spot maintained by Tuscarora State Forest. A short loop trail leads to a partially completed railroad tunnel with historic information at the trailhead. The park also provides access to the Iron Horse Trail for day and overnight hiking. The park takes its name from nearby Big Spring, whose waters form the scenic Shermans Creek.

Activities

❑ ATV/OHV	❑ Horseback Riding	❑ Fishing	❑ Wildlife
❑ Berry Picking	❑ Kayaking	❑ Hiking	❑ Bird Viewing
❑ Biking	❑ Photography	❑ Hunting	❑ Snowmobiling
❑ Boating	❑ Skiing	❑ Snowshoeing	❑ ....
❑ Canoeing	❑ Skijoring	❑ Swimming	❑ ....

Facilities

❑ ADA	❑ Visitor Center	❑ Museum	❑ ....
❑ Gift Shop	❑ Picnic Sites	❑ Restrooms	❑ ....

Notes

....
....
....
....

Passport Stamps

Black Moshannon State Park

Centre

DATE(S) VISITED:..

❑ SPRING   ❑ SUMMER   ❑ FALL   ❑ WINTER

WEATHER		TEMP:

☀ ❄☁ ☁ ☁🌧 ☁🌧 ☁🌨
❑   ❑   ❑   ❑   ❑   ❑

Check In:............................. Check Out:..............................

Lodging:................................... Park hours:........................

Who I Went With:...

Fee(s):.. Will I Return?   YES / NO

Rating ⭐⭐⭐⭐⭐

Activities

❑ ATV/OHV	❑ Horseback Riding	❑ Fishing	❑ Wildlife
❑ Berry Picking	❑ Kayaking	❑ Hiking	❑ Bird Viewing
❑ Biking	❑ Photography	❑ Hunting	❑ Snowmobiling
❑ Boating	❑ Skiing	❑ Snowshoeing	❑ ....
❑ Canoeing	❑ Skijoring	❑ Swimming	❑ ....

Facilities

❑ ADA	❑ Visitor Center	❑ Museum	❑ ....
❑ Gift Shop	❑ Picnic Sites	❑ Restrooms	❑ ....

Notes

....
....
....
....

Passport Stamps

Blue Knob State Park

DATE(S) VISITED:...

❏ SPRING ❏ SUMMER ❏ FALL ❏ WINTER

WEATHER	TEMP:

❏ ❏ ❏ ❏ ❏ ❏

Check In:............................ Check Out:............................

Lodging:.................................. Park hours:........................

Who I Went With:...

Fee(s):.................................. Will I Return? YES / NO

Rating ★ ★ ★ ★ ★

ABOUT THIS STATE PARK

Blue Knob State Park offers year-round wilderness adventures on 6,128 acres of woodland. The park is in the northwestern tip of Bedford County, west of I-99. Altoona, Johnstown, and Bedford are within 25 miles of this scenic park. One of the unique features of the park is the solitude it provides the visitor. There are many opportunities to enjoy the quiet and refreshing serenity of the mountains and streams.

Activities

❏ ATV/OHV	❏ Horseback Riding	❏ Fishing	❏ Wildlife
❏ Berry Picking	❏ Kayaking	❏ Hiking	❏ Bird Viewing
❏ Biking	❏ Photography	❏ Hunting	❏ Snowmobiling
❏ Boating	❏ Skiing	❏ Snowshoeing	❏ ....
❏ Canoeing	❏ Skijoring	❏ Swimming	❏ ....

Facilities

❏ ADA	❏ Visitor Center	❏ Museum	❏ ....
❏ Gift Shop	❏ Picnic Sites	❏ Restrooms	❏ ....

Notes

....
....
....
....

Passport Stamps

Boyd Big Tree Preserve Conservation Area

Dauphin

DATE(S) VISITED:..

❏ SPRING ❏ SUMMER ❏ FALL ❏ WINTER

WEATHER	TEMP:

☀ ❄ ☁ ☁ ☁🌧 ☁🌨 ☁❄
❏ ❏ ❏ ❏ ❏ ❏

Check In:............................. Check Out:.............................

Lodging:................................... Park hours:........................

Who I Went With:..

Fee(s):.. Will I Return? YES / NO

Rating ★ ★ ★ ★ ★

Activities

❏ ATV/OHV	❏ Horseback Riding	❏ Fishing	❏ Wildlife
❏ Berry Picking	❏ Kayaking	❏ Hiking	❏ Bird Viewing
❏ Biking	❏ Photography	❏ Hunting	❏ Snowmobiling
❏ Boating	❏ Skiing	❏ Snowshoeing	❏ ....
❏ Canoeing	❏ Skijoring	❏ Swimming	❏ ....

Facilities

❏ ADA	❏ Visitor Center	❏ Museum	❏ ....
❏ Gift Shop	❏ Picnic Sites	❏ Restrooms	❏ ....

Notes

....
....
....
....

Passport Stamps

Buchanan's Birthplace State Park

Franklin

DATE(S) VISITED:...

☐ SPRING ☐ SUMMER ☐ FALL ☐ WINTER

WEATHER			TEMP:

☐ ☐ ☐ ☐ ☐ ☐

Check In:................................ Check Out:................................

Lodging:................................ Park hours:........................

Who I Went With:...

Fee(s):.. Will I Return? YES / NO

Rating ★ ★ ★ ★ ★

ABOUT THIS STATE PARK

Buchanan's Birthplace State Park is an 18.5-acre park nestled in a gap of Tuscarora Mountain in Franklin County. The park and the surrounding forested mountains offer an abundance of beauty throughout the year. Buck Run flows through the park and hosts a population of native trout. Pennsylvania Fish and Boat Commission regulations and laws on approved trout waters apply to Buck Run.

Activities

☐ ATV/OHV	☐ Horseback Riding	☐ Fishing	☐ Wildlife
☐ Berry Picking	☐ Kayaking	☐ Hiking	☐ Bird Viewing
☐ Biking	☐ Photography	☐ Hunting	☐ Snowmobiling
☐ Boating	☐ Skiing	☐ Snowshoeing	☐ ....
☐ Canoeing	☐ Skijoring	☐ Swimming	☐ ....

Facilities

☐ ADA	☐ Visitor Center	☐ Museum	☐ ....
☐ Gift Shop	☐ Picnic Sites	☐ Restrooms	☐ ....

Notes

....
....
....
....

Passport Stamps

Bucktail State Park Natural Area

DATE(S) VISITED:..

❏ SPRING ❏ SUMMER ❏ FALL ❏ WINTER

WEATHER	TEMP:

☀ ❏ 🌤 ❏ ☁ ❏ 🌧 ❏ 🌧 ❏ 🌨 ❏

Check In:............................ Check Out:..............................

Lodging:.................................. Park hours:........................

Who I Went With:..

Fee(s):.. Will I Return?   YES / NO

Rating ★ ★ ★ ★ ★

ABOUT THIS STATE PARK

Bucktail State Park Natural Area provides a beautiful 75-mile scenic drive along PA 120 from Emporium, through Renovo, to Lock Haven. It stretches through a narrow valley known as the Bucktail Trail, named after the famous American Civil War regiment of Woodsmen, the Bucktails. The valley is mostly forested land with an occasional small village or isolated farm. This beautiful area has also been called the Bucktail Canyon because of the steep mountains that form beautiful forested walls.

Activities

❏ ATV/OHV	❏ Horseback Riding	❏ Fishing	❏ Wildlife
❏ Berry Picking	❏ Kayaking	❏ Hiking	❏ Bird Viewing
❏ Biking	❏ Photography	❏ Hunting	❏ Snowmobiling
❏ Boating	❏ Skiing	❏ Snowshoeing	❏ ....
❏ Canoeing	❏ Skijoring	❏ Swimming	❏ ....

Facilities

❏ ADA	❏ Visitor Center	❏ Museum	❏ ....
❏ Gift Shop	❏ Picnic Sites	❏ Restrooms	❏ ....

Notes

....
....
....
....

Passport Stamps

Caledonia State Park

DATE(S) VISITED:..

❏ SPRING ❏ SUMMER ❏ FALL ❏ WINTER

WEATHER					TEMP:
☀ ❏	☁ ❏	☁ ❏	☁ ❏	☁ ❏	☁ ❏

Check In:.............................. Check Out:..............................

Lodging:................................ Park hours:........................

Who I Went With:..

Fee(s):....................................... Will I Return? YES / NO

Rating ★ ★ ★ ★ ★

ABOUT THIS STATE PARK

The 1,125-acre Caledonia State Park is in Adams and Franklin counties. The park is nestled within South Mountain, the northern terminus of the well-known Blue Ridge Mountain of Maryland and Virginia. Within South Mountain there are four state parks and 84,000 acres of state forest land waiting to be explored and enjoyed. The soils on either side of South Mountain are ideal for fruit production, proven by the abundance of orchards in the surrounding area.

Activities

❏ ATV/OHV	❏ Horseback Riding	❏ Fishing	❏ Wildlife
❏ Berry Picking	❏ Kayaking	❏ Hiking	❏ Bird Viewing
❏ Biking	❏ Photography	❏ Hunting	❏ Snowmobiling
❏ Boating	❏ Skiing	❏ Snowshoeing	❏ ....
❏ Canoeing	❏ Skijoring	❏ Swimming	❏ ....

Facilities

❏ ADA	❏ Visitor Center	❏ Museum	❏ ....
❏ Gift Shop	❏ Picnic Sites	❏ Restrooms	❏ ....

Notes

....
....
....
....

Passport Stamps

Canoe Creek State Park

Blair

DATE(S) VISITED:..

❏ SPRING ❏ SUMMER ❏ FALL ❏ WINTER

WEATHER					TEMP:
☀	❄☁	☁	☁🌧	☁🌬	☁🌨
❏	❏	❏	❏	❏	❏

ABOUT THIS STATE PARK

The beautiful, 961-acre Canoe Creek State Park features a 155-acre lake, wetlands, old fields, and mature forests, which provide critical habitat for migrating birds and other wildlife. The lake is popular for fishing year round. Hikers enjoy the trails that wind through the many habitats. Picnicking, swimming at the beach, enjoying educational programs, and staying the night in a modern cabin also are popular activities.

Check In:............................. Check Out:...............................

Lodging:.................................. Park hours:........................

Who I Went With:..

Fee(s):.. Will I Return? YES / NO

Rating

⭐ ⭐ ⭐ ⭐ ⭐

Activities

❏ ATV/OHV
❏ Berry Picking
❏ Biking
❏ Boating
❏ Canoeing

❏ Horseback Riding
❏ Kayaking
❏ Photography
❏ Skiing
❏ Skijoring

❏ Fishing
❏ Hiking
❏ Hunting
❏ Snowshoeing
❏ Swimming

❏ Wildlife
❏ Bird Viewing
❏ Snowmobiling
❏ ....
❏ ....

Facilities

❏ ADA
❏ Gift Shop

❏ Visitor Center
❏ Picnic Sites

❏ Museum
❏ Restrooms

❏ ....
❏ ....

Notes

....
....
....
....

Passport Stamps

Chapman State Park

DATE(S) VISITED:..

☐ SPRING ☐ SUMMER ☐ FALL ☐ WINTER

WEATHER			TEMP:		
☐	☐	☐	☐	☐	☐

Check In:............................. Check Out:.............................

Lodging:............................. Park hours:.......................

Who I Went With:...

Fee(s):............................. Will I Return? YES / NO

Rating
★ ★ ★ ★ ★

ABOUT THIS STATE PARK

The 862-acre Chapman State Park includes the 68-acre Chapman Lake on the West Branch of Tionesta Creek. Adjacent to state game lands and the Allegheny National ForestOpens In A New Window, Chapman is an oasis of recreational facilities in a vast area of wilderness.

Activities

☐ ATV/OHV
☐ Berry Picking
☐ Biking
☐ Boating
☐ Canoeing

☐ Horseback Riding
☐ Kayaking
☐ Photography
☐ Skiing
☐ Skijoring

☐ Fishing
☐ Hiking
☐ Hunting
☐ Snowshoeing
☐ Swimming

☐ Wildlife
☐ Bird Viewing
☐ Snowmobiling
☐ ....
☐ ....

Facilities

☐ ADA
☐ Gift Shop

☐ Visitor Center
☐ Picnic Sites

☐ Museum
☐ Restrooms

☐ ....
☐ ....

Notes

....
....
....
....

Passport Stamps

Cherry Springs State Park

Potter

DATE(S) VISITED:..

☐ SPRING ☐ SUMMER ☐ FALL ☐ WINTER

WEATHER					TEMP:
☀ ☐	☁ ☐	☁ ☐	🌧 ☐	🌨 ☐	🌨 ☐

Check In:............................ Check Out:..............................

Lodging:.................................. Park hours:........................

Who I Went With:..

Fee(s):.. Will I Return? YES / NO

Rating ★ ★ ★ ★ ★

Activities

☐ ATV/OHV	☐ Horseback Riding	☐ Fishing	☐ Wildlife
☐ Berry Picking	☐ Kayaking	☐ Hiking	☐ Bird Viewing
☐ Biking	☐ Photography	☐ Hunting	☐ Snowmobiling
☐ Boating	☐ Skiing	☐ Snowshoeing	☐ ....
☐ Canoeing	☐ Skijoring	☐ Swimming	☐ ....

Facilities

☐ ADA	☐ Visitor Center	☐ Museum	☐ ....
☐ Gift Shop	☐ Picnic Sites	☐ Restrooms	☐ ....

Notes

....
....
....
....

Passport Stamps

Clear Creek State Park

DATE(S) VISITED:..

❑ SPRING   ❑ SUMMER   ❑ FALL   ❑ WINTER

WEATHER	TEMP:
☀ ❄☁ ☁ 🌧 🌧 🌨	
❑ ❑ ❑ ❑ ❑ ❑	

Check In:.............................. Check Out:..............................

Lodging:................................. Park hours:........................

Who I Went With:...

Fee(s):.. Will I Return? YES / NO

Rating ⭐ ⭐ ⭐ ⭐ ⭐

ABOUT THIS STATE PARK

Clear Creek State Park encompasses 1,901 acres in Jefferson County. The park occupies a scenic portion of the Clear Creek Valley from PA 949 to the Clarion River. The park has camping, rustic cabins, and Clarion River access for fishing and boating. Cook Forest State Park is only 11 miles away.

Activities

❑ ATV/OHV	❑ Horseback Riding	❑ Fishing	❑ Wildlife
❑ Berry Picking	❑ Kayaking	❑ Hiking	❑ Bird Viewing
❑ Biking	❑ Photography	❑ Hunting	❑ Snowmobiling
❑ Boating	❑ Skiing	❑ Snowshoeing	❑ ....
❑ Canoeing	❑ Skijoring	❑ Swimming	❑ ....

Facilities

❑ ADA	❑ Visitor Center	❑ Museum	❑ ....
❑ Gift Shop	❑ Picnic Sites	❑ Restrooms	❑ ....

Notes

....
....
....
....

Passport Stamps

Codorus State Park

DATE(S) VISITED:..

❑ SPRING ❑ SUMMER ❑ FALL ❑ WINTER

WEATHER			TEMP:		
❑	❑	❑	❑	❑	❑

Check In:............................ Check Out:...............................

Lodging:.................................. Park hours:.......................

Who I Went With:...

Fee(s):... Will I Return? YES / NO

Rating ⭐ ⭐ ⭐ ⭐ ⭐

ABOUT THIS STATE PARK

The 3,500-acre Codorus State Park is in the rolling hills of southern York County.The 1,275-acre Lake Marburg has 26 miles of shoreline and is a rest stop for migrating waterfowl and shorebirds. The lake is also popular with sail and motor boaters. Anglers love the lake for warmwater fishing and can also fish Codorus Creek for trout. Picnicking, swimming in the pool, and camping are popular activities.

Activities

❑ ATV/OHV	❑ Horseback Riding	❑ Fishing	❑ Wildlife
❑ Berry Picking	❑ Kayaking	❑ Hiking	❑ Bird Viewing
❑ Biking	❑ Photography	❑ Hunting	❑ Snowmobiling
❑ Boating	❑ Skiing	❑ Snowshoeing	❑ ....
❑ Canoeing	❑ Skijoring	❑ Swimming	❑ ....

Facilities

❑ ADA	❑ Visitor Center	❑ Museum	❑ ....
❑ Gift Shop	❑ Picnic Sites	❑ Restrooms	❑ ....

Notes

....
....
....
....

Passport Stamps

Colonel Denning State Park

Cumberland

DATE(S) VISITED:..

❑ SPRING ❑ SUMMER ❑ FALL ❑ WINTER

WEATHER	TEMP:
☀ ❄☁ ☁ ☁ ☁ ☁	
❑ ❑ ❑ ❑ ❑ ❑	

Check In:............................. Check Out:.............................

Lodging:.................................. Park hours:.......................

Who I Went With:...

Fee(s):... Will I Return? YES / NO

Rating ★ ★ ★ ★ ★

ABOUT THIS STATE PARK

Colonel Denning State Park, in north-central Cumberland County, has 273 acres of woodland and a 3.5-acre lake. The park serves as a gateway to the 96,000-acre Tuscarora State Forest, which surrounds the park. These scenic and historic public lands are located in Doubling Gap, so named by the "S" turn where Blue Mountain doubles back on itself.

Activities

❑ ATV/OHV   ❑ Horseback Riding   ❑ Fishing   ❑ Wildlife
❑ Berry Picking   ❑ Kayaking   ❑ Hiking   ❑ Bird Viewing
❑ Biking   ❑ Photography   ❑ Hunting   ❑ Snowmobiling
❑ Boating   ❑ Skiing   ❑ Snowshoeing   ❑ ....
❑ Canoeing   ❑ Skijoring   ❑ Swimming   ❑ ....

Facilities

❑ ADA   ❑ Visitor Center   ❑ Museum   ❑ ....
❑ Gift Shop   ❑ Picnic Sites   ❑ Restrooms   ❑ ....

Notes

....
....
....
....

Passport Stamps

Colton Point State Park

Tioga

DATE(S) VISITED:...

❑ SPRING ❑ SUMMER ❑ FALL ❑ WINTER

WEATHER		TEMP:

☀ ⛅ ☁ 🌧 🌨 🌨
❑ ❑ ❑ ❑ ❑ ❑

On the west rim of Pine Creek Gorge, also known as the Pennsylvania Grand Canyon, the 368-acre Colton Point State Park resonates with the rustic charm of the Civilian Conservation Corps era of the 1930s. The rugged overlooks offer great views of the canyon. Leonard Harrison State Park is visible on the other side of the canyon.

Check In:............................. Check Out:.............................

Lodging:.................................. Park hours:.......................

Who I Went With:...

Fee(s):.. Will I Return?   YES / NO

Rating ⭐ ⭐ ⭐ ⭐ ⭐

Activities

❑ ATV/OHV	❑ Horseback Riding	❑ Fishing	❑ Wildlife
❑ Berry Picking	❑ Kayaking	❑ Hiking	❑ Bird Viewing
❑ Biking	❑ Photography	❑ Hunting	❑ Snowmobiling
❑ Boating	❑ Skiing	❑ Snowshoeing	❑ ....
❑ Canoeing	❑ Skijoring	❑ Swimming	❑ ....

Facilities

❑ ADA	❑ Visitor Center	❑ Museum	❑ ....
❑ Gift Shop	❑ Picnic Sites	❑ Restrooms	❑ ....

Notes

....
....
....
....

Passport Stamps

Cook Forest State Park

Clarion, Fores, and Jefferson

DATE(S) VISITED:..

❑ SPRING   ❑ SUMMER   ❑ FALL   ❑ WINTER

WEATHER			TEMP:		
☀	⛅	☁	🌧	🌨	🌨
❑	❑	❑	❑	❑	❑

Check In:............................ Check Out:.............................

Lodging:.................................. Park hours:........................

Who I Went With:..

Fee(s):............................... Will I Return? YES / NO

Rating ★ ★ ★ ★ ★

ABOUT THIS STATE PARK

The 8,500-acre Cook Forest State Park and 3,136-acre Clarion River Lands lie in scenic northwestern Pennsylvania. Known for its stands of old growth forest, the park's Forest Cathedral of towering white pines and hemlocks is a National Natural Landmark. A scenic 13-mile stretch of the Clarion River flows through Cook Forest State Park and is popular for canoeing, kayaking, and tubing.

Activities

❑ ATV/OHV	❑ Horseback Riding	❑ Fishing	❑ Wildlife
❑ Berry Picking	❑ Kayaking	❑ Hiking	❑ Bird Viewing
❑ Biking	❑ Photography	❑ Hunting	❑ Snowmobiling
❑ Boating	❑ Skiing	❑ Snowshoeing	❑ ....
❑ Canoeing	❑ Skijoring	❑ Swimming	❑ ....

Facilities

❑ ADA	❑ Visitor Center	❑ Museum	❑ ....
❑ Gift Shop	❑ Picnic Sites	❑ Restrooms	❑ ....

Notes

....
....
....
....

Passport Stamps

Cowans Gap State Park

DATE(S) VISITED:...

❑ SPRING ❑ SUMMER ❑ FALL ❑ WINTER

WEATHER		TEMP:
☀ ❄☁ ☁ ☁ ☁ ☁		
❑ ❑ ❑ ❑ ❑ ❑		

Check In:............................. Check Out:...............................

Lodging:.................................. Park hours:........................

Who I Went With:..

Fee(s):.. Will I Return?   YES / NO

Rating ★ ★ ★ ★ ★

ABOUT THIS STATE PARK

Cowans Gap State Park is a 1,085-acre park in the beautiful Allens Valley of Fulton County. A 42-acre lake, large campground, rustic cabins, and many hiking trails are prime attractions. Buchanan State Forest surrounds the park, providing additional options for recreation and natural beauty in all seasons.

Activities

- ❑ ATV/OHV
- ❑ Berry Picking
- ❑ Biking
- ❑ Boating
- ❑ Canoeing
- ❑ Horseback Riding
- ❑ Kayaking
- ❑ Photography
- ❑ Skiing
- ❑ Skijoring
- ❑ Fishing
- ❑ Hiking
- ❑ Hunting
- ❑ Snowshoeing
- ❑ Swimming
- ❑ Wildlife
- ❑ Bird Viewing
- ❑ Snowmobiling
- ❑ ....
- ❑ ....

Facilities

- ❑ ADA
- ❑ Gift Shop
- ❑ Visitor Center
- ❑ Picnic Sites
- ❑ Museum
- ❑ Restrooms
- ❑ ....
- ❑ ....

Notes

....
....
....
....

Passport Stamps

Delaware Canal State Park

DATE(S) VISITED:..

❏ SPRING   ❏ SUMMER   ❏ FALL   ❏ WINTER

WEATHER						TEMP:
☀	✳☁	☁	☁☔	☁⚡	☁❄	
❏	❏	❏	❏	❏	❏	

Check In:............................ Check Out:............................

Lodging:................................ Park hours:........................

Who I Went With:..

Fee(s):.. Will I Return? YES / NO

Rating ★ ★ ★ ★ ★

ABOUT THIS STATE PARK

A walk along the 58.89-mile-long towpath of Delaware Canal State Park is a stroll into American history. Paralleling the Delaware River between Easton and Bristol, this diverse park contains: A historic canal and towpath, 50-acre pond, Many miles of river shoreline, 11 river islands including the Morgan Hill group (3), Loors, Whippoorwill, Old Sow, Raubs, Lynn/Frog/Rock group, and Hendricks

Activities

❏ ATV/OHV   ❏ Horseback Riding   ❏ Fishing   ❏ Wildlife
❏ Berry Picking   ❏ Kayaking   ❏ Hiking   ❏ Bird Viewing
❏ Biking   ❏ Photography   ❏ Hunting   ❏ Snowmobiling
❏ Boating   ❏ Skiing   ❏ Snowshoeing   ❏ ....
❏ Canoeing   ❏ Skijoring   ❏ Swimming   ❏ ....

Facilities

❏ ADA   ❏ Visitor Center   ❏ Museum   ❏ ....
❏ Gift Shop   ❏ Picnic Sites   ❏ Restrooms   ❏ ....

Notes

....
....
....
....

Passport Stamps

Denton Hill State Park

Potter

DATE(S) VISITED:...

☐ SPRING   ☐ SUMMER   ☐ FALL   ☐ WINTER

WEATHER		TEMP:
☀ ❄☁ ☁ ☁🌧 ☁🌧 ☁🌨		
☐ ☐ ☐ ☐ ☐ ☐		

Check In:.............................. Check Out:...............................

Lodging:.................................. Park hours:........................

Who I Went With:..

Fee(s):... Will I Return? YES / NO

Rating ⭐ ⭐ ⭐ ⭐ ⭐

Activities

☐ ATV/OHV	☐ Horseback Riding	☐ Fishing	☐ Wildlife
☐ Berry Picking	☐ Kayaking	☐ Hiking	☐ Bird Viewing
☐ Biking	☐ Photography	☐ Hunting	☐ Snowmobiling
☐ Boating	☐ Skiing	☐ Snowshoeing	☐ ....
☐ Canoeing	☐ Skijoring	☐ Swimming	☐ ....

Facilities

☐ ADA	☐ Visitor Center	☐ Museum	☐ ....
☐ Gift Shop	☐ Picnic Sites	☐ Restrooms	☐ ....

Notes

....
....
....
....

Passport Stamps

Elk State Park

DATE(S) VISITED:...

❑ SPRING   ❑ SUMMER   ❑ FALL   ❑ WINTER

WEATHER			TEMP:		
☀	❄☁	☁	☁	☁	☁
❑	❑	❑	❑	❑	❑

Check In:............................. Check Out:...........................

Lodging:................................. Park hours:........................

Who I Went With:..

Fee(s):.. Will I Return?   YES / NO

Rating
⭐ ⭐ ⭐ ⭐ ⭐

ABOUT THIS STATE PARK

Situated on the northern slope of Denton Hill, the park's elevation ranges from 1800 to 2400 feet above sea-level. The steep grade of the park facilitated the establishment of a downhill ski area and lodge when the site was developed in the 1950s and 1960s. Denton Hill State Park serves as a unique setting for a variety recreational events. Additionally, hikers can find year-round access to the Susquehannock State Forest -- Billy Lewis Area Trail System.

Activities

❑ ATV/OHV	❑ Horseback Riding	❑ Fishing	❑ Wildlife
❑ Berry Picking	❑ Kayaking	❑ Hiking	❑ Bird Viewing
❑ Biking	❑ Photography	❑ Hunting	❑ Snowmobiling
❑ Boating	❑ Skiing	❑ Snowshoeing	❑ ....
❑ Canoeing	❑ Skijoring	❑ Swimming	❑ ....

Facilities

❑ ADA	❑ Visitor Center	❑ Museum	❑ ....
❑ Gift Shop	❑ Picnic Sites	❑ Restrooms	❑ ....

Notes

....
....
....
....

Passport Stamps

Erie Bluffs State Park

DATE(S) VISITED:..

❏ SPRING ❏ SUMMER ❏ FALL ❏ WINTER

WEATHER	TEMP:

☀ 🌤 ☁ 🌧 🌧 🌨
❏ ❏ ❏ ❏ ❏ ❏

Check In:............................ Check Out:............................

Lodging:............................ Park hours:............................

Who I Went With:..

Fee(s):............................ Will I Return? YES / NO

Rating ⭐⭐⭐⭐⭐

ABOUT THIS STATE PARK

The 587-acre Erie Bluffs State Park lies along the Lake Erie shoreline in western Erie County, twelve miles west of the city of Erie. The park has: One mile of shoreline, 90-foot bluffs overlooking Lake Erie Elk Creek -- a shallow stream steelhead fishery, Several plant species of conservation concern, Uncommon black oak woodland/savannah Great Lakes region sand barren ecosystems, and Forested wetlands.

Activities

❏ ATV/OHV	❏ Horseback Riding	❏ Fishing	❏ Wildlife
❏ Berry Picking	❏ Kayaking	❏ Hiking	❏ Bird Viewing
❏ Biking	❏ Photography	❏ Hunting	❏ Snowmobiling
❏ Boating	❏ Skiing	❏ Snowshoeing	❏ ....
❏ Canoeing	❏ Skijoring	❏ Swimming	❏ ....

Facilities

❏ ADA	❏ Visitor Center	❏ Museum	❏ ....
❏ Gift Shop	❏ Picnic Sites	❏ Restrooms	❏ ....

Notes

....
....
....
....

Passport Stamps

Evansburg State Park

DATE(S) VISITED:...

❑ SPRING   ❑ SUMMER   ❑ FALL   ❑ WINTER

WEATHER			TEMP:		
❑	❑	❑	❑	❑	❑

Check In:............................. Check Out:...............................

Lodging:.................................. Park hours:.........................

Who I Went With:...

Fee(s):.. Will I Return? YES / NO

Rating ★ ★ ★ ★ ★

ABOUT THIS STATE PARK

Evansburg State Park is in southcentral Montgomery County between Norristown and Collegeville. Evansburg offers a significant area of green space and relative solitude in an urbanized area. The park is a quilt work of cropland, meadows, old fields, and mature woodlands that attracts day use visitors from the Montgomery County and Philadelphia areas. People come to the open play fields, picnic areas, trails, golf course, and the relatively tranquil, natural environment.

Activities

❑ ATV/OHV	❑ Horseback Riding	❑ Fishing	❑ Wildlife
❑ Berry Picking	❑ Kayaking	❑ Hiking	❑ Bird Viewing
❑ Biking	❑ Photography	❑ Hunting	❑ Snowmobiling
❑ Boating	❑ Skiing	❑ Snowshoeing	❑ ....
❑ Canoeing	❑ Skijoring	❑ Swimming	❑ ....

Facilities

❑ ADA	❑ Visitor Center	❑ Museum	❑ ....
❑ Gift Shop	❑ Picnic Sites	❑ Restrooms	❑ ....

Notes

....
....
....
....

Passport Stamps

Fort Washington State Park

Montgomery

DATE(S) VISITED:..

❑ SPRING ❑ SUMMER ❑ FALL ❑ WINTER

WEATHER	TEMP:

☀ ❑ ☁ ❑ ☁ ❑ ☔ ❑ ☔ ❑ ❄ ❑

Check In:............................. Check Out:...............................

Lodging:.................................... Park hours:..........................

Who I Went With:...

Fee(s):.. Will I Return? YES / NO

Rating ★ ★ ★ ★ ★

ABOUT THIS STATE PARK

Rich in modern recreational facilities and historical significance, Fort Washington blossoms with flowering dogwood in the spring. Fort Washington State Park consists of 493 acres in eastern Montgomery County. It takes its name from the temporary fort built by George Washington's troops in the fall of 1777, before heading to Valley Forge. The park is popular with hikers and picnickers. Birders enjoy the seasonal migration of raptors from the Observation Deck.

Activities

❑ ATV/OHV	❑ Horseback Riding	❑ Fishing	❑ Wildlife
❑ Berry Picking	❑ Kayaking	❑ Hiking	❑ Bird Viewing
❑ Biking	❑ Photography	❑ Hunting	❑ Snowmobiling
❑ Boating	❑ Skiing	❑ Snowshoeing	❑ ....
❑ Canoeing	❑ Skijoring	❑ Swimming	❑ ....

Facilities

❑ ADA	❑ Visitor Center	❑ Museum	❑ ....
❑ Gift Shop	❑ Picnic Sites	❑ Restrooms	❑ ....

Notes

....
....
....
....

Passport Stamps

Fowlers Hollow State Park

Perry

DATE(S) VISITED:..

❑ SPRING   ❑ SUMMER   ❑ FALL   ❑ WINTER

WEATHER		TEMP:			
☀ ❑	⛅ ❑	☁ ❑	🌧 ❑	🌧 ❑	🌨 ❑

Check In:............................. Check Out:.............................

Lodging:................................. Park hours:.......................

Who I Went With:...

Fee(s):.. Will I Return?   YES / NO

Rating ⭐ ⭐ ⭐ ⭐ ⭐

ABOUT THIS STATE PARK

The 104-acre Fowlers Hollow State Park is in a narrow valley created by Fowler Hollow Run. The park is on the edge of Tuscarora State Forest at the intersection of several multi-use trails. The campground of the park is a good base for adventures into the huge tract of public land.

Activities

❑ ATV/OHV	❑ Horseback Riding	❑ Fishing	❑ Wildlife
❑ Berry Picking	❑ Kayaking	❑ Hiking	❑ Bird Viewing
❑ Biking	❑ Photography	❑ Hunting	❑ Snowmobiling
❑ Boating	❑ Skiing	❑ Snowshoeing	❑ ....
❑ Canoeing	❑ Skijoring	❑ Swimming	❑ ....

Facilities

❑ ADA	❑ Visitor Center	❑ Museum	❑ ....
❑ Gift Shop	❑ Picnic Sites	❑ Restrooms	❑ ....

Notes

....
....
....
....

Passport Stamps

Frances Slocum State Park

Luzerne

DATE(S) VISITED:...

❏ SPRING   ❏ SUMMER   ❏ FALL   ❏ WINTER

WEATHER	TEMP:

❏ ❏ ❏ ❏ ❏ ❏

Check In:............................. Check Out:.............................

Lodging:................................. Park hours:.......................

Who I Went With:...

Fee(s):... Will I Return?   YES / NO

Rating ⭐ ⭐ ⭐ ⭐ ⭐

Activities

❏ ATV/OHV
❏ Berry Picking
❏ Biking
❏ Boating
❏ Canoeing

❏ Horseback Riding
❏ Kayaking
❏ Photography
❏ Skiing
❏ Skijoring

❏ Fishing
❏ Hiking
❏ Hunting
❏ Snowshoeing
❏ Swimming

❏ Wildlife
❏ Bird Viewing
❏ Snowmobiling
❏ ....
❏ ....

Facilities

❏ ADA
❏ Gift Shop

❏ Visitor Center
❏ Picnic Sites

❏ Museum
❏ Restrooms

❏ ....
❏ ....

Notes

....
....
....
....

Passport Stamps

French Creek State Park

DATE(S) VISITED:..

❏ SPRING ❏ SUMMER ❏ FALL ❏ WINTER

WEATHER			TEMP:		
❏	❏	❏	❏	❏	❏

Check In:.............................. Check Out:..............................

Lodging:.................................. Park hours:........................

Who I Went With:...

Fee(s):.. Will I Return? YES / NO

Rating ★ ★ ★ ★ ★

ABOUT THIS STATE PARK

Once an industrial complex for the fledgling United States of America, today French Creek State Park is an oasis for people and wildlife. Straddling the Schuylkill Highlands, the 7,730-acre park is the largest block of contiguous forest between Washington D.C. and New York City. The forests, lakes, wetlands, and fields are a destination for the people of southeast Pennsylvania to hike, fish, camp, and bike. Those same habitats are homes to many animals and plants that are rare.

Activities

❏ ATV/OHV	❏ Horseback Riding	❏ Fishing	❏ Wildlife
❏ Berry Picking	❏ Kayaking	❏ Hiking	❏ Bird Viewing
❏ Biking	❏ Photography	❏ Hunting	❏ Snowmobiling
❏ Boating	❏ Skiing	❏ Snowshoeing	❏ ....
❏ Canoeing	❏ Skijoring	❏ Swimming	❏ ....

Facilities

❏ ADA	❏ Visitor Center	❏ Museum	❏ ....
❏ Gift Shop	❏ Picnic Sites	❏ Restrooms	❏ ....

Notes

....
....
....
....

Passport Stamps

Gifford Pinchot State Park

York

DATE(S) VISITED:..

❏ SPRING   ❏ SUMMER   ❏ FALL   ❏ WINTER

WEATHER	TEMP:

❏   ❏   ❏   ❏   ❏   ❏

Check In:.............................. Check Out:...............................

Lodging:.................................... Park hours:........................

Who I Went With:...

Fee(s):.. Will I Return?   YES / NO

Rating ★ ★ ★ ★ ★

Activities

❏ ATV/OHV	❏ Horseback Riding	❏ Fishing	❏ Wildlife
❏ Berry Picking	❏ Kayaking	❏ Hiking	❏ Bird Viewing
❏ Biking	❏ Photography	❏ Hunting	❏ Snowmobiling
❏ Boating	❏ Skiing	❏ Snowshoeing	❏ ....
❏ Canoeing	❏ Skijoring	❏ Swimming	❏ ....

Facilities

❏ ADA	❏ Visitor Center	❏ Museum	❏ ....
❏ Gift Shop	❏ Picnic Sites	❏ Restrooms	❏ ....

Notes

....
....
....
....

Passport Stamps

Gouldsboro State Park

DATE(S) VISITED:..

❑ SPRING ❑ SUMMER ❑ FALL ❑ WINTER

WEATHER	TEMP:

☀ ☁ ☁ ☁ ☁ ☁
❑ ❑ ❑ ❑ ❑ ❑

Check In:............................. Check Out:.............................

Lodging:................................. Park hours:.......................

Who I Went With:..

Fee(s):................................... Will I Return? YES / NO

ABOUT THIS STATE PARK

Gouldsboro State Park, in Monroe and Wayne counties in northeastern Pennsylvania, contains 2,800 acres of land. The 250-acre Gouldsboro Lake is popular for fishing and boating.

Rating
⭐ ⭐ ⭐ ⭐ ⭐

Activities

❑ ATV/OHV	❑ Horseback Riding	❑ Fishing	❑ Wildlife
❑ Berry Picking	❑ Kayaking	❑ Hiking	❑ Bird Viewing
❑ Biking	❑ Photography	❑ Hunting	❑ Snowmobiling
❑ Boating	❑ Skiing	❑ Snowshoeing	❑ ....
❑ Canoeing	❑ Skijoring	❑ Swimming	❑ ....

Facilities

❑ ADA	❑ Visitor Center	❑ Museum	❑ ....
❑ Gift Shop	❑ Picnic Sites	❑ Restrooms	❑ ....

Notes
....
....
....
....

Passport Stamps

Greenwood Furnace State Park

Huntingdon

DATE(S) VISITED:..

☐ SPRING ☐ SUMMER ☐ FALL ☐ WINTER

WEATHER			TEMP:		
☀ ☐	⛅ ☐	☁ ☐	🌧 ☐	🌨 ☐	🌦 ☐

Check In:............................. Check Out:.............................

Lodging:............................. Park hours:.......................

Who I Went With:..

Fee(s):... Will I Return? YES / NO

Rating ⭐ ⭐ ⭐ ⭐ ⭐

ABOUT THIS STATE PARK

The park is on the western edge of the Seven Mountains in northeastern Huntingdon County, an area of rugged beauty, abundant wildlife, breathtaking vistas, and peaceful solitude. Greenwood Furnace State Park covers 423 acres, including a six-acre lake, campground, hiking trails, and a historic district. The park provides access to backpacking, hiking, mountain biking, hunting, and fishing in the surrounding 80,000-acre Rothrock State Forest.

Activities

☐ ATV/OHV	☐ Horseback Riding	☐ Fishing	☐ Wildlife
☐ Berry Picking	☐ Kayaking	☐ Hiking	☐ Bird Viewing
☐ Biking	☐ Photography	☐ Hunting	☐ Snowmobiling
☐ Boating	☐ Skiing	☐ Snowshoeing	☐ ....
☐ Canoeing	☐ Skijoring	☐ Swimming	☐ ....

Facilities

☐ ADA	☐ Visitor Center	☐ Museum	☐ ....
☐ Gift Shop	☐ Picnic Sites	☐ Restrooms	☐ ....

Notes

....
....
....
....

Passport Stamps

Hickory Run State Park

Carbon

DATE(S) VISITED:..

❑ SPRING ❑ SUMMER ❑ FALL ❑ WINTER

WEATHER			TEMP:		
☀	☁	☁	🌧	❄	🌨
❑	❑	❑	❑	❑	❑

The 15,990-acre Hickory Run State Park, Carbon County, lies in the western foothills of the Pocono Mountains. This large park has: More than 40 miles of hiking trails, Three state park natural areas, and Miles of trout streams. Boulder Field, a striking boulder-strewn area, is a National Natural Landmark.

Check In:............................. Check Out:.............................

Lodging:................................. Park hours:.......................

Who I Went With:..

Fee(s):.................................... Will I Return? YES / NO

Rating ⭐⭐⭐⭐⭐

Activities

❑ ATV/OHV   ❑ Horseback Riding   ❑ Fishing   ❑ Wildlife
❑ Berry Picking ❑ Kayaking   ❑ Hiking   ❑ Bird Viewing
❑ Biking   ❑ Photography   ❑ Hunting   ❑ Snowmobiling
❑ Boating   ❑ Skiing   ❑ Snowshoeing   ❑ ....
❑ Canoeing   ❑ Skijoring   ❑ Swimming   ❑ ....

Facilities

❑ ADA   ❑ Visitor Center   ❑ Museum   ❑ ....
❑ Gift Shop   ❑ Picnic Sites   ❑ Restrooms   ❑ ....

Notes

....
....
....
....

Passport Stamps

Hillman State Park

Washington

DATE(S) VISITED:..

☐ SPRING   ☐ SUMMER   ☐ FALL   ☐ WINTER

WEATHER	TEMP:

☀ ☐   ❄☁ ☐   ☁ ☐   ☁🌧 ☐   ☁ ☐   ☁ ☐

ABOUT THIS STATE PARK

This park is managed for hunting by the Pennsylvania Game Commission. Hiking trails are open to the public.

Check In:............................ Check Out:............................

Lodging:................................ Park hours:........................

Who I Went With:...

Fee(s):.. Will I Return?   YES / NO

Rating ⭐ ⭐ ⭐ ⭐ ⭐

Activities

☐ ATV/OHV   ☐ Horseback Riding   ☐ Fishing   ☐ Wildlife
☐ Berry Picking ☐ Kayaking   ☐ Hiking   ☐ Bird Viewing
☐ Biking   ☐ Photography   ☐ Hunting   ☐ Snowmobiling
☐ Boating   ☐ Skiing   ☐ Snowshoeing   ☐ ....
☐ Canoeing   ☐ Skijoring   ☐ Swimming   ☐ ....

Facilities

☐ ADA   ☐ Visitor Center   ☐ Museum   ☐ ....
☐ Gift Shop ☐ Picnic Sites   ☐ Restrooms   ☐ ....

Notes

....
....
....
....

Passport Stamps

Hills Creek State Park

Tioga

DATE(S) VISITED:..

☐ SPRING ☐ SUMMER ☐ FALL ☐ WINTER

WEATHER						TEMP:
☀	❄☁	☁	🌧	⛈	🌦	
☐	☐	☐	☐	☐	☐	

Check In:............................. Check Out:.............................

Lodging:................................. Park hours:.......................

Who I Went With:..

Fee(s):.................................. Will I Return? YES / NO

Rating ★ ★ ★ ★ ★

ABOUT THIS STATE PARK

Located in scenic Tioga County, the 407-acre Hills Creek State Park abounds in wildlife. Osprey, loon, and waterfowl visit the lake that boasts a variety of warmwater fish species. Camping, cabins, swimming, and picnicking make this an ideal spot for a family vacation.

Activities

☐ ATV/OHV
☐ Berry Picking
☐ Biking
☐ Boating
☐ Canoeing

☐ Horseback Riding
☐ Kayaking
☐ Photography
☐ Skiing
☐ Skijoring

☐ Fishing
☐ Hiking
☐ Hunting
☐ Snowshoeing
☐ Swimming

☐ Wildlife
☐ Bird Viewing
☐ Snowmobiling
☐ ....
☐ ....

Facilities

☐ ADA
☐ Gift Shop

☐ Visitor Center
☐ Picnic Sites

☐ Museum
☐ Restrooms

☐ ....
☐ ....

Notes

....
....
....
....

Passport Stamps

Hyner Run State Park

DATE(S) VISITED:..

❏ SPRING ❏ SUMMER ❏ FALL ❏ WINTER

WEATHER	TEMP:
☀ ❄☁ ☁ ☁ ☁ ☁	
❏ ❏ ❏ ❏ ❏ ❏	

Check In:.............................. Check Out:................................

Lodging:.................................. Park hours:.........................

Who I Went With:...

Fee(s):.. Will I Return? YES / NO

Rating ⭐⭐⭐⭐⭐

ABOUT THIS STATE PARK

Hyner Run carves a small valley from the surrounding steep mountains, creating a cozy, quiet place for outdoor adventures. The park is entirely surrounded by Sproul State Forest, Pennsylvania's largest state forest. Hyner View State Park also is nearby.

Activities

- ❏ ATV/OHV
- ❏ Berry Picking
- ❏ Biking
- ❏ Boating
- ❏ Canoeing
- ❏ Horseback Riding
- ❏ Kayaking
- ❏ Photography
- ❏ Skiing
- ❏ Skijoring
- ❏ Fishing
- ❏ Hiking
- ❏ Hunting
- ❏ Snowshoeing
- ❏ Swimming
- ❏ Wildlife
- ❏ Bird Viewing
- ❏ Snowmobiling
- ❏ ....
- ❏ ....

Facilities

- ❏ ADA
- ❏ Gift Shop
- ❏ Visitor Center
- ❏ Picnic Sites
- ❏ Museum
- ❏ Restrooms
- ❏ ....
- ❏ ....

Notes

....
....
....
....

Passport Stamps

Hyner View State Park

DATE(S) VISITED:..

❑ SPRING ❑ SUMMER ❑ FALL ❑ WINTER

WEATHER	TEMP:

☀ ❑ 🌤 ❑ ☁ ❑ 🌧 ❑ ⛈ ❑ 🌦 ❑

Check In:............................ Check Out:............................

Lodging:............................ Park hours:............................

Who I Went With:..

Fee(s):............................ Will I Return? YES / NO

Rating
⭐ ⭐ ⭐ ⭐ ⭐

ABOUT THIS STATE PARK

This small park features one of the nicest overlooks in DCNR's Bureau of State Parks and is popular for hang gliding. Hyner Run State Park is nearby. You can see vast distances both upstream and downstream over the West Branch of the Susquehanna River and surrounding mountains.

Activities

❑ ATV/OHV	❑ Horseback Riding	❑ Fishing	❑ Wildlife
❑ Berry Picking	❑ Kayaking	❑ Hiking	❑ Bird Viewing
❑ Biking	❑ Photography	❑ Hunting	❑ Snowmobiling
❑ Boating	❑ Skiing	❑ Snowshoeing	❑ ....
❑ Canoeing	❑ Skijoring	❑ Swimming	❑ ....

Facilities

❑ ADA	❑ Visitor Center	❑ Museum	❑ ....
❑ Gift Shop	❑ Picnic Sites	❑ Restrooms	❑ ....

Notes

....

....

....

....

Passport Stamps

Jacobsburg Environmental Education Center | Clinton

DATE(S) VISITED:..

❑ SPRING ❑ SUMMER ❑ FALL ❑ WINTER

WEATHER			TEMP:		
☀ ❑	☁ ❑	☁ ❑	🌧 ❑	🌨 ❑	🌨 ❑

Check In:............................ Check Out:............................

Lodging:................................ Park hours:......................

Who I Went With:..

Fee(s):... Will I Return? YES / NO

Rating ⭐ ⭐ ⭐ ⭐ ⭐

ABOUT THIS STATE PARK

Jacobsburg Environmental Education Center encompasses 1,168 acres of forests, fields, and creeks, which provide a wealth of recreational and educational opportunities. Visitors can enjoy exhibits at the visitor center during open hours, as well as Henrys Woods, an old growth forest surrounding Bushkill Creek, which has many hiking trails.

Activities

❑ ATV/OHV ❑ Horseback Riding ❑ Fishing ❑ Wildlife
❑ Berry Picking ❑ Kayaking ❑ Hiking ❑ Bird Viewing
❑ Biking ❑ Photography ❑ Hunting ❑ Snowmobiling
❑ Boating ❑ Skiing ❑ Snowshoeing ❑ ....
❑ Canoeing ❑ Skijoring ❑ Swimming ❑ ....

Facilities

❑ ADA ❑ Visitor Center ❑ Museum ❑ ....
❑ Gift Shop ❑ Picnic Sites ❑ Restrooms ❑ ....

Notes

....
....
....
....

Passport Stamps

DATE(S) VISITED:...

❏ SPRING   ❏ SUMMER   ❏ FALL   ❏ WINTER

WEATHER		TEMP:			
☀	⛅	☁	🌧	⛈	🌨
❏	❏	❏	❏	❏	❏

Check In:.............................. Check Out:..............................

Lodging:.................................. Park hours:........................

Who I Went With:...

Fee(s):.. Will I Return?   YES / NO

Rating ⭐ ⭐ ⭐ ⭐ ⭐

ABOUT THIS STATE PARK

Jennings Environmental Education Center is one of several state parks specifically dedicated to providing environmental education and recreational programs to the community. A variety of programs that increase knowledge and awareness of the beauty and importance of our natural resources are available for children, teachers, and the general public. Jennings provides a unique combination of prairie and forest environs, which offer a wide array of resource and educational opportunities.

Activities

❏ ATV/OHV	❏ Horseback Riding	❏ Fishing	❏ Wildlife
❏ Berry Picking	❏ Kayaking	❏ Hiking	❏ Bird Viewing
❏ Biking	❏ Photography	❏ Hunting	❏ Snowmobiling
❏ Boating	❏ Skiing	❏ Snowshoeing	❏ ....
❏ Canoeing	❏ Skijoring	❏ Swimming	❏ ....

Facilities

❏ ADA	❏ Visitor Center	❏ Museum	❏ ....
❏ Gift Shop	❏ Picnic Sites	❏ Restrooms	❏ ....

Notes

....
....
....
....

Passport Stamps

Joseph E. Ibberson Conservation Area   Dauphin

DATE(S) VISITED:..

❏ SPRING   ❏ SUMMER   ❏ FALL   ❏ WINTER

WEATHER	TEMP:

☀ 🌤 ☁ 🌧 🌧 🌨
❏   ❏   ❏   ❏   ❏   ❏

Check In:............................ Check Out:..............................

Lodging:.................................. Park hours:........................

Who I Went With:...

Fee(s):... Will I Return?   YES / NO

Rating ★ ★ ★ ★ ★

Activities

❏ ATV/OHV	❏ Horseback Riding	❏ Fishing	❏ Wildlife
❏ Berry Picking	❏ Kayaking	❏ Hiking	❏ Bird Viewing
❏ Biking	❏ Photography	❏ Hunting	❏ Snowmobiling
❏ Boating	❏ Skiing	❏ Snowshoeing	❏ ....
❏ Canoeing	❏ Skijoring	❏ Swimming	❏ ....

Facilities

❏ ADA	❏ Visitor Center	❏ Museum	❏ ....
❏ Gift Shop	❏ Picnic Sites	❏ Restrooms	❏ ....

Notes

....
....
....
....

Passport Stamps

Kettle Creek State Park

Clinton

DATE(S) VISITED:..

❑ SPRING   ❑ SUMMER   ❑ FALL   ❑ WINTER

WEATHER	TEMP:

☀ ❄☁ ☁ ☁🌧 ☁🌨 ☁

❑   ❑   ❑   ❑   ❑   ❑

Check In:............................. Check Out:..............................

Lodging:.................................. Park hours:........................

Who I Went With:..

Fee(s):.. Will I Return? YES / NO

Rating ⭐ ⭐ ⭐ ⭐ ⭐

Activities

❑ ATV/OHV   ❑ Horseback Riding   ❑ Fishing   ❑ Wildlife
❑ Berry Picking ❑ Kayaking   ❑ Hiking   ❑ Bird Viewing
❑ Biking   ❑ Photography   ❑ Hunting   ❑ Snowmobiling
❑ Boating   ❑ Skiing   ❑ Snowshoeing   ❑ ....
❑ Canoeing   ❑ Skijoring   ❑ Swimming   ❑ ....

Facilities

❑ ADA   ❑ Visitor Center   ❑ Museum   ❑ ....
❑ Gift Shop   ❑ Picnic Sites   ❑ Restrooms   ❑ ....

Notes

....
....
....
....

Passport Stamps

Keystone State Park

DATE(S) VISITED:...................................

❑ SPRING   ❑ SUMMER   ❑ FALL   ❑ WINTER

WEATHER					TEMP:
☀ ✳☁	☁	☁	☁ |||||	☁ ⚡	☁ ⋰
❑	❑	❑	❑	❑	❑

ABOUT THIS STATE PARK

The 1,200-acre Keystone State Park is great for day-trips and family vacations year round. Camping, modern cabins, many trails, and a lake are all within walking distance, providing an ideal setting for wildlife watching or outdoor adventures. The park is within easy driving distance from the Pittsburgh metropolitan area, the Laurel Highlands, and their many attractions.

Check In:............................. Check Out:..............................

Lodging:.................................. Park hours:........................

Who I Went With:...

Fee(s):............................. Will I Return?   YES / NO

Rating   ★ ★ ★ ★ ★

Activities

❑ ATV/OHV   ❑ Horseback Riding   ❑ Fishing   ❑ Wildlife
❑ Berry Picking ❑ Kayaking   ❑ Hiking   ❑ Bird Viewing
❑ Biking   ❑ Photography   ❑ Hunting   ❑ Snowmobiling
❑ Boating   ❑ Skiing   ❑ Snowshoeing   ❑ ....
❑ Canoeing   ❑ Skijoring   ❑ Swimming   ❑ ....

Facilities

❑ ADA   ❑ Visitor Center   ❑ Museum   ❑ ....
❑ Gift Shop   ❑ Picnic Sites   ❑ Restrooms   ❑ ....

Notes
....
....
....
....

Passport Stamps

DATE(S) VISITED:..

☐ SPRING   ☐ SUMMER   ☐ FALL   ☐ WINTER

WEATHER					TEMP:
☀	❄☁	☁	☁|||||	☁⋰	☁⋰
☐	☐	☐	☐	☐	☐

Check In:............................. Check Out:.............................

Lodging:.................................. Park hours:........................

Who I Went With:..

Fee(s):... Will I Return?   YES / NO

Rating   ★ ★ ★ ★ ★

ABOUT THIS STATE PARK

Kings Gap Environmental Education Center's unique attractions are its mountainous terrain, extensive forest, and panoramic views, which may be experienced while driving the winding road to the mansion area. The sweeping view of the Cumberland Valley from the Cameron-Masland Mansion is impressive at any time of the year. Kings Gap consists of 2,531 acres of forest on South Mountain, with more than 25 miles of hiking trails, a permanent orienteering course, picnicking, hunting, and other recreational and educational opportunities.

Activities

☐ ATV/OHV   ☐ Horseback Riding   ☐ Fishing   ☐ Wildlife
☐ Berry Picking   ☐ Kayaking   ☐ Hiking   ☐ Bird Viewing
☐ Biking   ☐ Photography   ☐ Hunting   ☐ Snowmobiling
☐ Boating   ☐ Skiing   ☐ Snowshoeing   ☐ ....
☐ Canoeing   ☐ Skijoring   ☐ Swimming   ☐ ....

Facilities

☐ ADA   ☐ Visitor Center   ☐ Museum   ☐ ....
☐ Gift Shop ☐ Picnic Sites   ☐ Restrooms   ☐ ....

Notes

....
....
....
....

Passport Stamps

Kinzua Bridge State Park

McKean

DATE(S) VISITED:..

❏ SPRING   ❏ SUMMER   ❏ FALL   ❏ WINTER

WEATHER	TEMP:
☀ ❄☁ ☁ ☁||||| ☁⚊ ☁⋯	
❏ ❏ ❏ ❏ ❏ ❏	

Check In:............................ Check Out:.............................

Lodging:................................ Park hours:........................

Who I Went With:..

Fee(s):.......................... Will I Return?   YES / NO

Rating ★ ★ ★ ★ ★

Activities

❏ ATV/OHV	❏ Horseback Riding	❏ Fishing	❏ Wildlife
❏ Berry Picking	❏ Kayaking	❏ Hiking	❏ Bird Viewing
❏ Biking	❏ Photography	❏ Hunting	❏ Snowmobiling
❏ Boating	❏ Skiing	❏ Snowshoeing	❏ ....
❏ Canoeing	❏ Skijoring	❏ Swimming	❏ ....

Facilities

❏ ADA	❏ Visitor Center	❏ Museum	❏ ....
❏ Gift Shop	❏ Picnic Sites	❏ Restrooms	❏ ....

Notes

....
....
....
....

Passport Stamps

Kooser State Park

DATE(S) VISITED:...

❑ SPRING   ❑ SUMMER   ❑ FALL   ❑ WINTER

WEATHER		TEMP:

☀ ❄☁ ☁ ☁|||| ☁💧 ☁

❑   ❑   ❑   ❑   ❑   ❑

ABOUT THIS STATE PARK

In the heart of the Laurel Highlands at an altitude of 2,600 feet, Kooser State Park attracts visitors all year to its 250 acres of forest and the beautiful trout stream that flows the full length of the park.
The park's basic appeal lies in its intimate areas which are best suited for family outings and small groups. Picnicking, fishing, hiking, camping, cross-country skiing, and family cabins are popular.

Check In:............................. Check Out:.............................

Lodging:............................. Park hours:.......................

Who I Went With:...

Fee(s):.. Will I Return?   YES / NO

Rating ★ ★ ★ ★ ★

Activities

❑ ATV/OHV	❑ Horseback Riding	❑ Fishing	❑ Wildlife
❑ Berry Picking	❑ Kayaking	❑ Hiking	❑ Bird Viewing
❑ Biking	❑ Photography	❑ Hunting	❑ Snowmobiling
❑ Boating	❑ Skiing	❑ Snowshoeing	❑ ....
❑ Canoeing	❑ Skijoring	❑ Swimming	❑ ....

Facilities

❑ ADA	❑ Visitor Center	❑ Museum	❑ ....
❑ Gift Shop	❑ Picnic Sites	❑ Restrooms	❑ ....

Notes

....
....
....
....

Passport Stamps

Lackawanna State Park

Lackawanna

DATE(S) VISITED:..

❏ SPRING   ❏ SUMMER   ❏ FALL   ❏ WINTER

WEATHER	TEMP:

❏   ❏   ❏   ❏   ❏   ❏

Check In:.............................. Check Out:................................

Lodging:................................. Park hours:........................

Who I Went With:..

Fee(s):.. Will I Return?   YES / NO

Rating ★★★★★

ABOUT THIS STATE PARK

The 1,445-acre Lackawanna State Park is in northeastern Pennsylvania, ten miles north of Scranton. The centerpiece of the park, the 198-acre Lackawanna Lake, is surrounded by picnic areas and multi-use trails winding through forest. Boating, camping, fishing, mountain biking, and swimming are popular recreation activities.

Activities

❏ ATV/OHV	❏ Horseback Riding	❏ Fishing	❏ Wildlife
❏ Berry Picking	❏ Kayaking	❏ Hiking	❏ Bird Viewing
❏ Biking	❏ Photography	❏ Hunting	❏ Snowmobiling
❏ Boating	❏ Skiing	❏ Snowshoeing	❏ ....
❏ Canoeing	❏ Skijoring	❏ Swimming	❏ ....

Facilities

❏ ADA	❏ Visitor Center	❏ Museum	❏ ....
❏ Gift Shop	❏ Picnic Sites	❏ Restrooms	❏ ....

Notes

....
....
....
....

Passport Stamps

Laurel Hill State Park

DATE(S) VISITED:..

❑ SPRING   ❑ SUMMER   ❑ FALL   ❑ WINTER

WEATHER	TEMP:
☀ ❑ ❄☁ ❑ ☁ ❑ ☁ |||||| ❑ ☁ ☷ ❑ ☁ ⋯ ❑	

Check In:.............................. Check Out:.............................

Lodging:.................................. Park hours:.......................

Who I Went With:..

Fee(s):.. Will I Return?   YES / NO

Rating ★ ★ ★ ★ ★

ABOUT THIS STATE PARK

Laurel Hill State Park consists of 4,062 acres of mountainous terrain in Somerset County. The 63-acre Laurel Hill Lake is a focal point of the park. Laurel Hill is surrounded by thousands of acres of pristine state park and state forest lands. A trail system invites visitors to explore the park and observe the diversity of plants and wildlife. The Jones Mill Run Dam and the Hemlock Trail Natural Area are two must-see destinations on your visit.

Activities

❑ ATV/OHV	❑ Horseback Riding	❑ Fishing	❑ Wildlife
❑ Berry Picking	❑ Kayaking	❑ Hiking	❑ Bird Viewing
❑ Biking	❑ Photography	❑ Hunting	❑ Snowmobiling
❑ Boating	❑ Skiing	❑ Snowshoeing	❑ ....
❑ Canoeing	❑ Skijoring	❑ Swimming	❑ ....

Facilities

❑ ADA	❑ Visitor Center	❑ Museum	❑ ....
❑ Gift Shop	❑ Picnic Sites	❑ Restrooms	❑ ....

Notes

....
....
....
....

Passport Stamps

Laurel Ridge State Park

Somerset and Westmoreland

DATE(S) VISITED:..

❑ SPRING ❑ SUMMER ❑ FALL ❑ WINTER

WEATHER	TEMP:
☀ ⛅ ☁ 🌧 ⛈ 🌨	
❑ ❑ ❑ ❑ ❑ ❑	

Check In:............................ Check Out:..............................

Lodging:.................................. Park hours:........................

Who I Went With:..

Fee(s):... Will I Return? YES / NO

Rating ★ ★ ★ ★ ★

Activities

❑ ATV/OHV	❑ Horseback Riding	❑ Fishing	❑ Wildlife
❑ Berry Picking	❑ Kayaking	❑ Hiking	❑ Bird Viewing
❑ Biking	❑ Photography	❑ Hunting	❑ Snowmobiling
❑ Boating	❑ Skiing	❑ Snowshoeing	❑ ....
❑ Canoeing	❑ Skijoring	❑ Swimming	❑ ....

Facilities

❑ ADA	❑ Visitor Center	❑ Museum	❑ ....
❑ Gift Shop	❑ Picnic Sites	❑ Restrooms	❑ ....

Notes

....
....
....
....

Passport Stamps

Laurel Mountain State Park

DATE(S) VISITED:...

❑ SPRING　❑ SUMMER　❑ FALL　❑ WINTER

WEATHER	TEMP:

❑　❑　❑　❑　❑　❑

ABOUT THIS STATE PARK

The 13,625-acre Laurel Ridge State Park stretches along Laurel Mountain from the picturesque Youghiogheny River at Ohiopyle, to the Conemaugh Gorge near Johnstown. This large park spans Cambria, Fayette, Somerset, and Westmoreland counties. The main feature of the park is the 70-mile Laurel Highlands Hiking Trail, which provides the setting for a semi-wilderness backpacking and day hiking experience.

Check In:............................. Check Out:.............................

Lodging:................................... Park hours:........................

Who I Went With:..

Fee(s):... Will I Return?　YES / NO

Rating　★ ★ ★ ★ ★

Activities

❑ ATV/OHV　　❑ Horseback Riding　❑ Fishing　❑ Wildlife

❑ Berry Picking　❑ Kayaking　　❑ Hiking　❑ Bird Viewing

❑ Biking　　❑ Photography　❑ Hunting　❑ Snowmobiling

❑ Boating　　❑ Skiing　　❑ Snowshoeing　❑ ....

❑ Canoeing　❑ Skijoring　❑ Swimming　❑ ....

Facilities

❑ ADA　　❑ Visitor Center　❑ Museum　❑ ....

❑ Gift Shop　❑ Picnic Sites　❑ Restrooms　❑ ....

Notes

....
....
....
....

Passport Stamps

Laurel Summit State Park

DATE(S) VISITED:..

❑ SPRING   ❑ SUMMER   ❑ FALL   ❑ WINTER

WEATHER			TEMP:		
☀	⛅	☁	🌧	🌨	🌨
❑	❑	❑	❑	❑	❑

Check In:.............................. Check Out:.............................

Lodging:.................................. Park hours:.......................

Who I Went With:..

Fee(s):... Will I Return?   YES / NO

Rating ★ ★ ★ ★ ★

ABOUT THIS STATE PARK

This scenic picnic area is operated by the DCNR's Bureau of State Parks. The six-acre area offers picnic tables, a pavilion, water, and restroom. The area is 2,739 feet above sea level and several degrees cooler than surrounding towns. This area also provides trailhead parking for Spruce Flats bog and Wolf Rocks Trail.

Activities

❑ ATV/OHV	❑ Horseback Riding	❑ Fishing	❑ Wildlife
❑ Berry Picking	❑ Kayaking	❑ Hiking	❑ Bird Viewing
❑ Biking	❑ Photography	❑ Hunting	❑ Snowmobiling
❑ Boating	❑ Skiing	❑ Snowshoeing	❑ ....
❑ Canoeing	❑ Skijoring	❑ Swimming	❑ ....

Facilities

❑ ADA	❑ Visitor Center	❑ Museum	❑ ....
❑ Gift Shop	❑ Picnic Sites	❑ Restrooms	❑ ....

Notes

....
....
....
....

Passport Stamps

Lehigh Gorge State Park

DATE(S) VISITED:...

❏ SPRING   ❏ SUMMER   ❏ FALL   ❏ WINTER

WEATHER					TEMP:
❏	❏	❏	❏	❏	❏

Check In:............................ Check Out:...............................

Lodging:................................. Park hours:.....................

Who I Went With:...

Fee(s):... Will I Return? YES / NO

Rating ★ ★ ★ ★ ★

ABOUT THIS STATE PARK

A deep, steep-walled gorge carved by a river, thick vegetation, rock outcroppings, and waterfalls characterize Lehigh Gorge State Park
The 6,107 acres of park land follow the Lehigh River from Francis E. Walter Dam in the north to Jim Thorpe in the south. Whitewater boating and biking are popular activities. The abandoned railroad grade along the river provides opportunities for hiking, bicycling, sightseeing, and photography.

Activities

❏ ATV/OHV	❏ Horseback Riding	❏ Fishing	❏ Wildlife
❏ Berry Picking	❏ Kayaking	❏ Hiking	❏ Bird Viewing
❏ Biking	❏ Photography	❏ Hunting	❏ Snowmobiling
❏ Boating	❏ Skiing	❏ Snowshoeing	❏ ....
❏ Canoeing	❏ Skijoring	❏ Swimming	❏ ....

Facilities

❏ ADA	❏ Visitor Center	❏ Museum	❏ ....
❏ Gift Shop	❏ Picnic Sites	❏ Restrooms	❏ ....

Notes

....
....
....
....

Passport Stamps

Leonard Harrison State Park

DATE(S) VISITED:..

❑ SPRING ❑ SUMMER ❑ FALL ❑ WINTER

WEATHER	TEMP:

❑ ❑ ❑ ❑ ❑ ❑

ABOUT THIS STATE PARK

On the east rim of the canyon, the 585-acre Leonard Harrison State Park has modern facilities, a visitor center, and the most famous scenic views of the canyon. On the other side of the canyon is Colton Point State Park.

Check In:.............................. Check Out:..............................

Lodging:................................. Park hours:........................

Who I Went With:..

Fee(s):.. Will I Return?   YES / NO

Rating ★ ★ ★ ★ ★

Activities

❑ ATV/OHV
❑ Berry Picking
❑ Biking
❑ Boating
❑ Canoeing

❑ Horseback Riding
❑ Kayaking
❑ Photography
❑ Skiing
❑ Skijoring

❑ Fishing
❑ Hiking
❑ Hunting
❑ Snowshoeing
❑ Swimming

❑ Wildlife
❑ Bird Viewing
❑ Snowmobiling
❑ ....
❑ ....

Facilities

❑ ADA
❑ Gift Shop

❑ Visitor Center
❑ Picnic Sites

❑ Museum
❑ Restrooms

❑ ....
❑ ....

Notes

....
....
....
....

Passport Stamps

Linn Run State Park

Westmorelan

DATE(S) VISITED:...

❑ SPRING ❑ SUMMER ❑ FALL ❑ WINTER

WEATHER				TEMP:	
☀	❄☁	☁	🌧	🌧	🌨
❑	❑	❑	❑	❑	❑

Check In:............................ Check Out:...............................

Lodging:.................................... Park hours:.........................

Who I Went With:..

Fee(s):... Will I Return? YES / NO

Rating ★ ★ ★ ★ ★

ABOUT THIS STATE PARK

The varied topography and mixed hardwood and evergreen forest make the 612-acre Linn Run State Park a scenic place for picnicking, hiking, and cabin rentals. Grove and Rock runs join to make Linn Run, an excellent trout stream. A lovely waterfall, Adam Falls, is a scenic spot nearby the picnic area. Forbes State Forest borders Linn Run State Park and offers 50,000 acres of land for outdoor recreation.

Activities

❑ ATV/OHV	❑ Horseback Riding	❑ Fishing	❑ Wildlife
❑ Berry Picking	❑ Kayaking	❑ Hiking	❑ Bird Viewing
❑ Biking	❑ Photography	❑ Hunting	❑ Snowmobiling
❑ Boating	❑ Skiing	❑ Snowshoeing	❑ ....
❑ Canoeing	❑ Skijoring	❑ Swimming	❑ ....

Facilities

❑ ADA	❑ Visitor Center	❑ Museum	❑ ....
❑ Gift Shop	❑ Picnic Sites	❑ Restrooms	❑ ....

Notes

....

....

....

....

Passport Stamps

Little Buffalo State Park

Perry

DATE(S) VISITED:..

❑ SPRING ❑ SUMMER ❑ FALL ❑ WINTER

WEATHER	TEMP:
☀ ❄ ☁ ☁ ☁ ☁ ☁	
❑ ❑ ❑ ❑ ❑ ❑	

Check In:............................. Check Out:...............................

Lodging:................................... Park hours:........................

Who I Went With:..

Fee(s):.. Will I Return?   YES / NO

Rating ★★★★★

Activities

❑ ATV/OHV   ❑ Horseback Riding   ❑ Fishing   ❑ Wildlife
❑ Berry Picking ❑ Kayaking   ❑ Hiking   ❑ Bird Viewing
❑ Biking   ❑ Photography   ❑ Hunting   ❑ Snowmobiling
❑ Boating   ❑ Skiing   ❑ Snowshoeing ❑ ....
❑ Canoeing   ❑ Skijoring   ❑ Swimming   ❑ ....

Facilities

❑ ADA   ❑ Visitor Center ❑ Museum   ❑ ....
❑ Gift Shop ❑ Picnic Sites   ❑ Restrooms ❑ ....

Notes

....
....
....
....

Passport Stamps

Little Pine State Park

DATE(S) VISITED:..

❑ SPRING ❑ SUMMER ❑ FALL ❑ WINTER

WEATHER	TEMP:

❑ ❑ ❑ ❑ ❑ ❑

ABOUT THIS STATE PARK

The 2,158-acre Little Pine State Park is surrounded by a beautiful mountain section of Tiadaghton State Forest in the Pennsylvania WildsOpens In A New Window. The 45-acre Little Pine Lake, hiking trails, campground, and nesting bald eagles are prime attractions to the park.

Check In:.............................. Check Out:..............................

Lodging:.................................. Park hours:........................

Who I Went With:...

Fee(s):.. Will I Return? YES / NO

Rating ★ ★ ★ ★ ★

Activities

❑ ATV/OHV	❑ Horseback Riding	❑ Fishing	❑ Wildlife
❑ Berry Picking	❑ Kayaking	❑ Hiking	❑ Bird Viewing
❑ Biking	❑ Photography	❑ Hunting	❑ Snowmobiling
❑ Boating	❑ Skiing	❑ Snowshoeing	❑ ....
❑ Canoeing	❑ Skijoring	❑ Swimming	❑ ....

Facilities

❑ ADA	❑ Visitor Center	❑ Museum	❑ ....
❑ Gift Shop	❑ Picnic Sites	❑ Restrooms	❑ ....

Notes

....
....
....
....

Passport Stamps

Locust Lake State Park

Schuylkill

DATE(S) VISITED:..

☐ SPRING   ☐ SUMMER   ☐ FALL   ☐ WINTER

WEATHER	TEMP:
☀ ☁ ☁ ☁ ☁ ☁	
☐ ☐ ☐ ☐ ☐ ☐	

Check In:............................ Check Out:...............................

Lodging:................................. Park hours:........................

Who I Went With:...

Fee(s):.. Will I Return?   YES / NO

Rating ⭐ ⭐ ⭐ ⭐ ⭐

ABOUT THIS STATE PARK

Known for its popular camping area, Locust Lake State Park nestles on the side of Locust Mountain. The 52-acre Locust Lake is located between two campgrounds and is surrounded by beautiful forests. Hiking and fishing are popular activities in the 1,772-acre park.

Activities

☐ ATV/OHV	☐ Horseback Riding	☐ Fishing	☐ Wildlife
☐ Berry Picking	☐ Kayaking	☐ Hiking	☐ Bird Viewing
☐ Biking	☐ Photography	☐ Hunting	☐ Snowmobiling
☐ Boating	☐ Skiing	☐ Snowshoeing	☐ ....
☐ Canoeing	☐ Skijoring	☐ Swimming	☐ ....

Facilities

☐ ADA	☐ Visitor Center	☐ Museum	☐ ....
☐ Gift Shop	☐ Picnic Sites	☐ Restrooms	☐ ....

Notes

....

....

....

....

Passport Stamps

Locust Lake State Park

DATE(S) VISITED:...

❏ SPRING   ❏ SUMMER   ❏ FALL   ❏ WINTER

WEATHER	TEMP:
☀ ❄☁ ☁ ☁ ☁ ☁	
❏ ❏ ❏ ❏ ❏ ❏	

Check In:............................. Check Out:.............................

Lodging:............................. Park hours:.........................

Who I Went With:..

Fee(s):....................................... Will I Return?   YES / NO

Rating ★ ★ ★ ★ ★

ABOUT THIS STATE PARK

The 595-acre Lyman Run State Park is in scenic Potter County. Maples and cherries dominate a mixed northern hardwood forest that surrounds the 45-acre Lyman Run Lake, making a most scenic setting.

Activities

❏ ATV/OHV	❏ Horseback Riding	❏ Fishing	❏ Wildlife
❏ Berry Picking	❏ Kayaking	❏ Hiking	❏ Bird Viewing
❏ Biking	❏ Photography	❏ Hunting	❏ Snowmobiling
❏ Boating	❏ Skiing	❏ Snowshoeing	❏ ....
❏ Canoeing	❏ Skijoring	❏ Swimming	❏ ....

Facilities

❏ ADA	❏ Visitor Center	❏ Museum	❏ ....
❏ Gift Shop	❏ Picnic Sites	❏ Restrooms	❏ ....

Notes

....
....
....
....

Passport Stamps

Lyman Run State Park

Potter

DATE(S) VISITED:...

❏ SPRING ❏ SUMMER ❏ FALL ❏ WINTER

WEATHER	TEMP:

☀ ❏   ⛅ ❏   ☁ ❏   🌧 ❏   🌦 ❏   🌨 ❏

Check In:................................ Check Out:..............................

Lodging:................................ Park hours:........................

Who I Went With:..

Fee(s):.. Will I Return? YES / NO

Rating ⭐ ⭐ ⭐ ⭐ ⭐

ABOUT THIS STATE PARK

The 595-acre Lyman Run State Park is in scenic Potter County. Maples and cherries dominate a mixed northern hardwood forest that surrounds the 45-acre Lyman Run Lake, making a most scenic setting.

Activities

❏ ATV/OHV	❏ Horseback Riding	❏ Fishing	❏ Wildlife
❏ Berry Picking	❏ Kayaking	❏ Hiking	❏ Bird Viewing
❏ Biking	❏ Photography	❏ Hunting	❏ Snowmobiling
❏ Boating	❏ Skiing	❏ Snowshoeing	❏ ....
❏ Canoeing	❏ Skijoring	❏ Swimming	❏ ....

Facilities

❏ ADA	❏ Visitor Center	❏ Museum	❏ ....
❏ Gift Shop	❏ Picnic Sites	❏ Restrooms	❏ ....

Notes

....
....
....
....

Passport Stamps

Marsh Creek State Park

DATE(S) VISITED:..

❑ SPRING   ❑ SUMMER   ❑ FALL   ❑ WINTER

WEATHER	TEMP:

❑   ❑   ❑   ❑   ❑   ❑

Check In:............................. Check Out:...............................

Lodging:.................................... Park hours:........................

Who I Went With:...

Fee(s):.. Will I Return?   YES / NO

Rating ⭐ ⭐ ⭐ ⭐ ⭐

ABOUT THIS STATE PARK

Marsh Creek State Park is in the rolling hills of north central Chester County. The 1,784-acre park contains the 535-acre Marsh Creek Lake, which is a wonderful resource for fishing, sailing, and migrating waterfowl.

Activities

❑ ATV/OHV	❑ Horseback Riding	❑ Fishing	❑ Wildlife
❑ Berry Picking	❑ Kayaking	❑ Hiking	❑ Bird Viewing
❑ Biking	❑ Photography	❑ Hunting	❑ Snowmobiling
❑ Boating	❑ Skiing	❑ Snowshoeing	❑ ....
❑ Canoeing	❑ Skijoring	❑ Swimming	❑ ....

Facilities

❑ ADA	❑ Visitor Center	❑ Museum	❑ ....
❑ Gift Shop	❑ Picnic Sites	❑ Restrooms	❑ ....

Notes

....
....
....
....

Passport Stamps

Maurice K. Goddard State Park

Mercer

DATE(S) VISITED:...

❑ SPRING   ❑ SUMMER   ❑ FALL   ❑ WINTER

WEATHER	TEMP:

❑ ❑ ❑ ❑ ❑ ❑

Check In:.............................. Check Out:...............................

Lodging:.................................. Park hours:........................

Who I Went With:...

Fee(s):.. Will I Return?   YES / NO

Rating ★ ★ ★ ★ ★

Activities

❑ ATV/OHV   ❑ Horseback Riding   ❑ Fishing   ❑ Wildlife
❑ Berry Picking ❑ Kayaking   ❑ Hiking   ❑ Bird Viewing
❑ Biking   ❑ Photography   ❑ Hunting   ❑ Snowmobiling
❑ Boating   ❑ Skiing   ❑ Snowshoeing   ❑ ....
❑ Canoeing   ❑ Skijoring   ❑ Swimming   ❑ ....

Facilities

❑ ADA   ❑ Visitor Center   ❑ Museum   ❑ ....
❑ Gift Shop   ❑ Picnic Sites   ❑ Restrooms   ❑ ....

Notes

....
....
....
....

Passport Stamps

McCalls Dam State Park

Centre

DATE(S) VISITED:...

❑ SPRING   ❑ SUMMER   ❑ FALL   ❑ WINTER

WEATHER		TEMP:			
❑	❑	❑	❑	❑	❑

Check In:............................. Check Out:..............................

Lodging:.................................. Park hours:........................

Who I Went With:...

Fee(s):.. Will I Return? YES / NO

Rating ★ ★ ★ ★ ★

ABOUT THIS STATE PARK

The sound of White Deer Creek pervades the quiet, remote McCalls Dam State Park. Majestic pines, hemlocks, maples, and oaks reach for the sky around the small picnic area. Bald Eagle State Forest surrounds the eight-acre McCalls Dam State Park.

Activities

❑ ATV/OHV	❑ Horseback Riding	❑ Fishing	❑ Wildlife
❑ Berry Picking	❑ Kayaking	❑ Hiking	❑ Bird Viewing
❑ Biking	❑ Photography	❑ Hunting	❑ Snowmobiling
❑ Boating	❑ Skiing	❑ Snowshoeing	❑ ....
❑ Canoeing	❑ Skijoring	❑ Swimming	❑ ....

Facilities

❑ ADA	❑ Visitor Center	❑ Museum	❑ ....
❑ Gift Shop	❑ Picnic Sites	❑ Restrooms	❑ ....

Notes

....
....
....
....

Passport Stamps

McConnells Mill State Park

Lawrence

DATE(S) VISITED:..

❏ SPRING   ❏ SUMMER   ❏ FALL   ❏ WINTER

WEATHER		TEMP:

❏   ❏   ❏   ❏   ❏   ❏

ABOUT THIS STATE PARK

McConnells Mill State Park, in Lawrence County, encompasses 2,546 acres of the spectacular Slippery Rock Creek Gorge, which is a National Natural Landmark. Created by the draining of glacial lakes thousands of years ago, the gorge has steep sides while the valley floor is littered with huge boulders. Scenic overlooks and waterfalls are popular natural attractions. Visitors can tour a historic gristmill and covered bridge built in the 1800s.

Check In:............................. Check Out:.............................

Lodging:................................. Park hours:.........................

Who I Went With:...

Fee(s):... Will I Return?   YES / NO

Rating ★ ★ ★ ★ ★

Activities

❏ ATV/OHV   ❏ Horseback Riding   ❏ Fishing   ❏ Wildlife
❏ Berry Picking   ❏ Kayaking   ❏ Hiking   ❏ Bird Viewing
❏ Biking   ❏ Photography   ❏ Hunting   ❏ Snowmobiling
❏ Boating   ❏ Skiing   ❏ Snowshoeing   ❏ ....
❏ Canoeing   ❏ Skijoring   ❏ Swimming   ❏ ....

Facilities

❏ ADA   ❏ Visitor Center   ❏ Museum   ❏ ....
❏ Gift Shop   ❏ Picnic Sites   ❏ Restrooms   ❏ ....

Notes

....
....
....
....

Passport Stamps

Memorial Lake State Park

DATE(S) VISITED:..

❏ SPRING   ❏ SUMMER   ❏ FALL   ❏ WINTER

WEATHER	TEMP:

☀ ❏   ❏   ❏   ❏   ❏   ❏

Check In:............................. Check Out:.........................

Lodging:................................ Park hours:......................

Who I Went With:...

Fee(s):... Will I Return? YES / NO

Rating ⭐ ⭐ ⭐ ⭐ ⭐

ABOUT THIS STATE PARK

Memorial Lake State Park's 230 acres are near the base of Blue Mountain in East Hanover Township, Lebanon County. The park is surrounded by Fort Indiantown Gap, the headquarters for the Pennsylvania Army and Air National Guard.

Activities

❏ ATV/OHV	❏ Horseback Riding	❏ Fishing	❏ Wildlife
❏ Berry Picking	❏ Kayaking	❏ Hiking	❏ Bird Viewing
❏ Biking	❏ Photography	❏ Hunting	❏ Snowmobiling
❏ Boating	❏ Skiing	❏ Snowshoeing	❏ ....
❏ Canoeing	❏ Skijoring	❏ Swimming	❏ ....

Facilities

❏ ADA	❏ Visitor Center	❏ Museum	❏ ....
❏ Gift Shop	❏ Picnic Sites	❏ Restrooms	❏ ....

Notes

....
....
....
....

Passport Stamps

Memorial Lake State Park

Lebanon

DATE(S) VISITED:...

☐ SPRING ☐ SUMMER ☐ FALL ☐ WINTER

WEATHER	TEMP:
☀ ☐ 🌤 ☐ ☁ ☐ 🌧 ☐ 🌧 ☐ 🌨 ☐	

Check In:............................ Check Out:..............................

Lodging:.................................. Park hours:.......................

Who I Went With:...

Fee(s):.. Will I Return? YES / NO

Rating ★ ★ ★ ★ ★

ABOUT THIS STATE PARK

Memorial Lake State Park's 230 acres are near the base of Blue Mountain in East Hanover Township, Lebanon County. The park is surrounded by Fort Indiantown Gap, the headquarters for the Pennsylvania Army and Air National Guard.

Activities

☐ ATV/OHV
☐ Berry Picking
☐ Biking
☐ Boating
☐ Canoeing

☐ Horseback Riding
☐ Kayaking
☐ Photography
☐ Skiing
☐ Skijoring

☐ Fishing
☐ Hiking
☐ Hunting
☐ Snowshoeing
☐ Swimming

☐ Wildlife
☐ Bird Viewing
☐ Snowmobiling
☐ ....
☐ ....

Facilities

☐ ADA
☐ Gift Shop

☐ Visitor Center
☐ Picnic Sites

☐ Museum
☐ Restrooms

☐ ....
☐ ....

Notes

....
....
....
....

Passport Stamps

Memorial Lake State Park

Lebanon

DATE(S) VISITED:..

❑ SPRING ❑ SUMMER ❑ FALL ❑ WINTER

WEATHER	TEMP:
☀ ❑ ❄☁ ❑ ☁ ❑ ☁🌧 ❑ ☁🌧 ❑ ☁🌨 ❑	

Check In:............................. Check Out:.............................

Lodging:................................. Park hours:.......................

Who I Went With:..

Fee(s):............................. Will I Return? YES / NO

Rating ⭐⭐⭐⭐⭐

ABOUT THIS STATE PARK

Memorial Lake State Park's 230 acres are near the base of Blue Mountain in East Hanover Township, Lebanon County. The park is surrounded by Fort Indiantown Gap, the headquarters for the Pennsylvania Army and Air National Guard.

Activities

❑ ATV/OHV	❑ Horseback Riding	❑ Fishing	❑ Wildlife
❑ Berry Picking	❑ Kayaking	❑ Hiking	❑ Bird Viewing
❑ Biking	❑ Photography	❑ Hunting	❑ Snowmobiling
❑ Boating	❑ Skiing	❑ Snowshoeing	❑ ....
❑ Canoeing	❑ Skijoring	❑ Swimming	❑ ....

Facilities

❑ ADA	❑ Visitor Center	❑ Museum	❑ ....
❑ Gift Shop	❑ Picnic Sites	❑ Restrooms	❑ ....

Notes

....
....
....
....

Passport Stamps

Milton State Park

DATE(S) VISITED:..

❏ SPRING ❏ SUMMER ❏ FALL ❏ WINTER

WEATHER			TEMP:		
☀	☁	☁	☁	☁	☁
❏	❏	❏	❏	❏	❏

Check In:............................. Check Out:..............................

Lodging:................................. Park hours:........................

Who I Went With:...

Fee(s):.. Will I Return? YES / NO

Rating ★ ★ ★ ★ ★

ABOUT THIS STATE PARK

Milton State Park is an 82-acre island on the West Branch Susquehanna River, between the boroughs of Milton and West Milton. The northern half of the park has day use facilities and the southern half remains in a wooded state for hiking and nature study.

Activities

❏ ATV/OHV	❏ Horseback Riding	❏ Fishing	❏ Wildlife
❏ Berry Picking	❏ Kayaking	❏ Hiking	❏ Bird Viewing
❏ Biking	❏ Photography	❏ Hunting	❏ Snowmobiling
❏ Boating	❏ Skiing	❏ Snowshoeing	❏ ....
❏ Canoeing	❏ Skijoring	❏ Swimming	❏ ....

Facilities

❏ ADA	❏ Visitor Center	❏ Museum	❏ ....
❏ Gift Shop	❏ Picnic Sites	❏ Restrooms	❏ ....

Notes

....
....
....
....

Passport Stamps

Mont Alto State Park

Franklin

DATE(S) VISITED:...

❑ SPRING ❑ SUMMER ❑ FALL ❑ WINTER

| WEATHER | TEMP: |

❑ ❑ ❑ ❑ ❑ ❑

Check In:............................ Check Out:...............................

Lodging:.................................. Park hours:........................

Who I Went With:..

Fee(s):.. Will I Return? YES / NO

Rating ⭐ ⭐ ⭐ ⭐ ⭐

ABOUT THIS STATE PARK

Milton State Park is an 82-acre island on the West Branch Susquehanna River, between the boroughs of Milton and West Milton. The northern half of the park has day use facilities and the southern half remains in a wooded state for hiking and nature study.

Activities

- ❑ ATV/OHV
- ❑ Berry Picking
- ❑ Biking
- ❑ Boating
- ❑ Canoeing
- ❑ Horseback Riding
- ❑ Kayaking
- ❑ Photography
- ❑ Skiing
- ❑ Skijoring
- ❑ Fishing
- ❑ Hiking
- ❑ Hunting
- ❑ Snowshoeing
- ❑ Swimming
- ❑ Wildlife
- ❑ Bird Viewing
- ❑ Snowmobiling
- ❑ ....
- ❑ ....

Facilities

- ❑ ADA
- ❑ Gift Shop
- ❑ Visitor Center
- ❑ Picnic Sites
- ❑ Museum
- ❑ Restrooms
- ❑ ....
- ❑ ....

Notes

....
....
....
....

Passport Stamps

Mont Alto State Park

Franklin

DATE(S) VISITED:..

❑ SPRING   ❑ SUMMER   ❑ FALL   ❑ WINTER

WEATHER	TEMP:

☀ ❄☁ ☁ ☔ ⛈ 🌨
❑   ❑   ❑   ❑   ❑   ❑

Check In:............................ Check Out:............................

Lodging:............................ Park hours:........................

Who I Went With:..

Fee(s):... Will I Return? YES / NO

Rating ★★★★★

Activities

❑ ATV/OHV   ❑ Horseback Riding   ❑ Fishing   ❑ Wildlife
❑ Berry Picking   ❑ Kayaking   ❑ Hiking   ❑ Bird Viewing
❑ Biking   ❑ Photography   ❑ Hunting   ❑ Snowmobiling
❑ Boating   ❑ Skiing   ❑ Snowshoeing   ❑ ....
❑ Canoeing   ❑ Skijoring   ❑ Swimming   ❑ ....

Facilities

❑ ADA   ❑ Visitor Center   ❑ Museum   ❑ ....
❑ Gift Shop   ❑ Picnic Sites   ❑ Restrooms   ❑ ....

Notes

....
....
....
....

Passport Stamps

Mont Alto State Park

Franklin

DATE(S) VISITED:...

❑ SPRING ❑ SUMMER ❑ FALL ❑ WINTER

WEATHER	TEMP:

☀ ❆☁ ☁ ☁🌧 ☁🌧 ☁🌨
❑ ❑ ❑ ❑ ❑ ❑

Check In:............................. Check Out:.............................

Lodging:................................. Park hours:........................

Who I Went With:..

Fee(s):.. Will I Return? YES / NO

ABOUT THIS STATE PARK

This quiet, 24-acre park features a unique pavilion, picnicking, and trout fishing. Mont Alto is the oldest park still in the Pennsylvania state park system.

Rating ⭐ ⭐ ⭐ ⭐ ⭐

Activities

❑ ATV/OHV	❑ Horseback Riding	❑ Fishing	❑ Wildlife
❑ Berry Picking	❑ Kayaking	❑ Hiking	❑ Bird Viewing
❑ Biking	❑ Photography	❑ Hunting	❑ Snowmobiling
❑ Boating	❑ Skiing	❑ Snowshoeing	❑ ....
❑ Canoeing	❑ Skijoring	❑ Swimming	❑ ....

Facilities

❑ ADA	❑ Visitor Center	❑ Museum	❑ ....
❑ Gift Shop	❑ Picnic Sites	❑ Restrooms	❑ ....

Notes

....

....

....

....

Passport Stamps

Moraine State Park

Butler

DATE(S) VISITED:...

❑ SPRING　　❑ SUMMER　　❑ FALL　　❑ WINTER

WEATHER			TEMP:		
☀	☁	☁	☁	☁	☁
❑	❑	❑	❑	❑	❑

Check In:............................ Check Out:..............................

Lodging:................................... Park hours:........................

Who I Went With:..

Fee(s):.. Will I Return?　YES / NO

Rating ⭐ ⭐ ⭐ ⭐ ⭐

Activities

❑ ATV/OHV	❑ Horseback Riding	❑ Fishing	❑ Wildlife
❑ Berry Picking	❑ Kayaking	❑ Hiking	❑ Bird Viewing
❑ Biking	❑ Photography	❑ Hunting	❑ Snowmobiling
❑ Boating	❑ Skiing	❑ Snowshoeing	❑ ....
❑ Canoeing	❑ Skijoring	❑ Swimming	❑ ....

Facilities

❑ ADA	❑ Visitor Center	❑ Museum	❑ ....
❑ Gift Shop	❑ Picnic Sites	❑ Restrooms	❑ ....

Notes

....
....
....
....

Passport Stamps

Mt. Pisgah State Park

DATE(S) VISITED:...

❑ SPRING   ❑ SUMMER   ❑ FALL   ❑ WINTER

WEATHER	TEMP:

☀ ❑   ⛅ ❑   ☁ ❑   🌧 ❑   ⛈ ❑   🌨 ❑

Check In:............................. Check Out:.............................

Lodging:.................................. Park hours:........................

Who I Went With:..

Fee(s):.. Will I Return?   YES / NO

Rating
★ ★ ★ ★ ★

ABOUT THIS STATE PARK

Mount Pisgah State Park is in the scenic Endless Mountains region of Pennsylvania's Northern Tier. Midway between Troy and Towanda in Bradford County, the 1,302-acre park is along Mill Creek, at the base of Mt. Pisgah, elevation 2,260 feet. A dam on Mill Creek forms Stephen Foster Lake, named after the famous composer and onetime local resident. The 75-acre lake provides fishing, boating, and skating.

Activities

❑ ATV/OHV	❑ Horseback Riding	❑ Fishing	❑ Wildlife
❑ Berry Picking	❑ Kayaking	❑ Hiking	❑ Bird Viewing
❑ Biking	❑ Photography	❑ Hunting	❑ Snowmobiling
❑ Boating	❑ Skiing	❑ Snowshoeing	❑ ....
❑ Canoeing	❑ Skijoring	❑ Swimming	❑ ....

Facilities

❑ ADA	❑ Visitor Center	❑ Museum	❑ ....
❑ Gift Shop	❑ Picnic Sites	❑ Restrooms	❑ ....

Notes

....
....
....
....

Passport Stamps

Nescopeck State Park

Luzerne

DATE(S) VISITED:..

❑ SPRING   ❑ SUMMER   ❑ FALL   ❑ WINTER

WEATHER		TEMP:	
☀ ❑	🌤 ❑	☁ ❑	🌧 ❑	🌧 ❑	🌨 ❑

Check In:............................ Check Out:...............................

Lodging:.................................. Park hours:........................

Who I Went With:...

Fee(s):.. Will I Return?   YES / NO

Rating ⭐ ⭐ ⭐ ⭐ ⭐

Bordered on the south by steep Mount Yeager and on the north by Nescopeck Mountain, the 3,550-acre Nescopeck State Park encompasses wetlands, rich forests, and many diverse habitats. Nescopeck Creek, a favorite of anglers, meanders through the park. Hiking trails follow the creek, pass through quiet forests, and skirt wetlands. Interpretive exhibits highlighting the park's natural history can be seen inside the environmental education center.

Activities

❑ ATV/OHV	❑ Horseback Riding	❑ Fishing	❑ Wildlife
❑ Berry Picking	❑ Kayaking	❑ Hiking	❑ Bird Viewing
❑ Biking	❑ Photography	❑ Hunting	❑ Snowmobiling
❑ Boating	❑ Skiing	❑ Snowshoeing	❑ ....
❑ Canoeing	❑ Skijoring	❑ Swimming	❑ ....

Facilities

❑ ADA	❑ Visitor Center	❑ Museum	❑ ....
❑ Gift Shop	❑ Picnic Sites	❑ Restrooms	❑ ....

Notes

....
....
....
....

Passport Stamps

Neshaminy State Park

DATE(S) VISITED:...

☐ SPRING ☐ SUMMER ☐ FALL ☐ WINTER

WEATHER						TEMP:
☀	❄☁	☁	☁ |||||	☁ 💧	☁ ⋰
☐	☐	☐	☐	☐	☐

Check In:............................. Check Out:.............................

Lodging:............................. Park hours:.......................

Who I Went With:...

Fee(s):............................. Will I Return? YES / NO

Rating ⭐⭐⭐⭐⭐

ABOUT THIS STATE PARK

Neshaminy State Park is along the Delaware River in lower Bucks County. The park takes its name from Neshaminy Creek, which joins the Delaware River at this point. The park's 339 acres include picnic areas, a swimming pool, and a separate children's spray park. Boating access to the Delaware River is provided at the marina.

Activities

- ☐ ATV/OHV
- ☐ Berry Picking
- ☐ Biking
- ☐ Boating
- ☐ Canoeing

- ☐ Horseback Riding
- ☐ Kayaking
- ☐ Photography
- ☐ Skiing
- ☐ Skijoring

- ☐ Fishing
- ☐ Hiking
- ☐ Hunting
- ☐ Snowshoeing
- ☐ Swimming

- ☐ Wildlife
- ☐ Bird Viewing
- ☐ Snowmobiling
- ☐ ....
- ☐ ....

Facilities

- ☐ ADA
- ☐ Gift Shop

- ☐ Visitor Center
- ☐ Picnic Sites

- ☐ Museum
- ☐ Restrooms

- ☐ ....
- ☐ ....

Notes

....
....
....
....

Passport Stamps

Nockamixon State Park

Bucks

DATE(S) VISITED:..

❑ SPRING ❑ SUMMER ❑ FALL ❑ WINTER

WEATHER	TEMP:
☀ ❄☁ ☁ ☁|||| ☁🌧 ☁❄	
❑ ❑ ❑ ❑ ❑ ❑	

Check In:............................ Check Out:..............................

Lodging:............................ Park hours:........................

Who I Went With:...

Fee(s):.. Will I Return? YES / NO

Rating ⭐ ⭐ ⭐ ⭐ ⭐

Activities

❑ ATV/OHV	❑ Horseback Riding	❑ Fishing	❑ Wildlife
❑ Berry Picking	❑ Kayaking	❑ Hiking	❑ Bird Viewing
❑ Biking	❑ Photography	❑ Hunting	❑ Snowmobiling
❑ Boating	❑ Skiing	❑ Snowshoeing	❑ ....
❑ Canoeing	❑ Skijoring	❑ Swimming	❑ ....

Facilities

❑ ADA	❑ Visitor Center	❑ Museum	❑ ....
❑ Gift Shop	❑ Picnic Sites	❑ Restrooms	❑ ....

Notes

....
....
....
....

Passport Stamps

DATE(S) VISITED:...

❑ SPRING   ❑ SUMMER   ❑ FALL   ❑ WINTER

WEATHER	TEMP:

☀ ❑   ⛅ ❑   ☁ ❑   🌧 ❑   ⛈ ❑   🌨 ❑

Check In:.............................. Check Out:..............................

Lodging:................................. Park hours:........................

Who I Went With:...

Fee(s):... Will I Return?   YES / NO

Rating ★ ★ ★ ★ ★

ABOUT THIS STATE PARK

Nolde Forest encompasses more than 725 acres of deciduous woodlands and coniferous plantations. A network of trails makes the center's streams, ponds, and diverse habitats accessible to both students and visitors. Teaching stations offer places for students to work and benches for those who wish to sit and enjoy the sights and sounds of the natural world. ADA accessible trails are located at the Nolde Mansion and historic sawmill.

Activities

❑ ATV/OHV	❑ Horseback Riding	❑ Fishing	❑ Wildlife
❑ Berry Picking	❑ Kayaking	❑ Hiking	❑ Bird Viewing
❑ Biking	❑ Photography	❑ Hunting	❑ Snowmobiling
❑ Boating	❑ Skiing	❑ Snowshoeing	❑ ....
❑ Canoeing	❑ Skijoring	❑ Swimming	❑ ....

Facilities

❑ ADA	❑ Visitor Center	❑ Museum	❑ ....
❑ Gift Shop	❑ Picnic Sites	❑ Restrooms	❑ ....

Notes

....
....
....
....

Passport Stamps

Norristown Farm Park

Montgomery

DATE(S) VISITED:...

☐ SPRING   ☐ SUMMER   ☐ FALL   ☐ WINTER

WEATHER	TEMP:

☐ ☐ ☐ ☐ ☐ ☐

Check In:............................. Check Out:...............................

Lodging:................................. Park hours:........................

Who I Went With:..

Fee(s):... Will I Return?   YES / NO

Rating   ★ ★ ★ ★ ★

Activities

☐ ATV/OHV   ☐ Horseback Riding   ☐ Fishing   ☐ Wildlife
☐ Berry Picking   ☐ Kayaking   ☐ Hiking   ☐ Bird Viewing
☐ Biking   ☐ Photography   ☐ Hunting   ☐ Snowmobiling
☐ Boating   ☐ Skiing   ☐ Snowshoeing   ☐ ....
☐ Canoeing   ☐ Skijoring   ☐ Swimming   ☐ ....

Facilities

☐ ADA   ☐ Visitor Center   ☐ Museum   ☐ ....
☐ Gift Shop   ☐ Picnic Sites   ☐ Restrooms   ☐ ....

Notes

....
....
....
....

Passport Stamps

Ohiopyle State Park

DATE(S) VISITED:..

❑ SPRING   ❑ SUMMER   ❑ FALL   ❑ WINTER

WEATHER				TEMP:	
☀	❄☁	☁	☁‖‖	☁	☁
❑	❑	❑	❑	❑	❑

Check In:.............................. Check Out:..............................

Lodging:.................................. Park hours:........................

Who I Went With:...

Fee(s):.. Will I Return?   YES / NO

Rating ★ ★ ★ ★ ★

ABOUT THIS STATE PARK

Located on the southern reaches of the Laurel Ridge, Ohiopyle State Park encompasses approximately 20,500 acres of rugged natural beauty and serves as the gateway to the Laurel Highlands. Close to major metropolitan areas and offering vast choices of activities,
Passing through the heart of the park, the rushing waters of the Youghiogheny [yawki-gay-nee] River Gorge are the centerpiece for Ohiopyle. The "Yough" [yawk] provides some of the best whitewater boating in the eastern United States.

Activities

❑ ATV/OHV	❑ Horseback Riding	❑ Fishing	❑ Wildlife
❑ Berry Picking	❑ Kayaking	❑ Hiking	❑ Bird Viewing
❑ Biking	❑ Photography	❑ Hunting	❑ Snowmobiling
❑ Boating	❑ Skiing	❑ Snowshoeing	❑ ....
❑ Canoeing	❑ Skijoring	❑ Swimming	❑ ....

Facilities

❑ ADA	❑ Visitor Center	❑ Museum	❑ ....
❑ Gift Shop	❑ Picnic Sites	❑ Restrooms	❑ ....

Notes

....
....
....
....

Passport Stamps

Oil Creek State Park

Venango

DATE(S) VISITED:..

❏ SPRING   ❏ SUMMER   ❏ FALL   ❏ WINTER

WEATHER	TEMP:

❏   ❏   ❏   ❏   ❏   ❏

Check In:.............................. Check Out:..............................

Lodging:.................................. Park hours:........................

Who I Went With:...

Fee(s):... Will I Return?   YES / NO

Rating ★ ★ ★ ★ ★

Activities

❏ ATV/OHV	❏ Horseback Riding	❏ Fishing	❏ Wildlife
❏ Berry Picking	❏ Kayaking	❏ Hiking	❏ Bird Viewing
❏ Biking	❏ Photography	❏ Hunting	❏ Snowmobiling
❏ Boating	❏ Skiing	❏ Snowshoeing	❏ ....
❏ Canoeing	❏ Skijoring	❏ Swimming	❏ ....

Facilities

❏ ADA	❏ Visitor Center	❏ Museum	❏ ....
❏ Gift Shop	❏ Picnic Sites	❏ Restrooms	❏ ....

Notes
....
....
....
....

Passport Stamps

Ole Bull State Park

Potter

DATE(S) VISITED:..

❑ SPRING   ❑ SUMMER   ❑ FALL   ❑ WINTER

WEATHER		TEMP:

☀ ❄☁ ☁ 🌧 🌦 🌨
❑ ❑ ❑ ❑ ❑ ❑

Ole Bull State Park consists of 132 acres along the Kettle Creek Valley in Potter County. This area is called the Black Forest because of its once dense tree cover, mountainous terrain, and wilderness habitat.

Check In:............................ Check Out:............................

Lodging:............................ Park hours:........................

Who I Went With:..

Fee(s):.. Will I Return?   YES / NO

Rating ⭐ ⭐ ⭐ ⭐ ⭐

Activities

❑ ATV/OHV   ❑ Horseback Riding   ❑ Fishing   ❑ Wildlife
❑ Berry Picking   ❑ Kayaking   ❑ Hiking   ❑ Bird Viewing
❑ Biking   ❑ Photography   ❑ Hunting   ❑ Snowmobiling
❑ Boating   ❑ Skiing   ❑ Snowshoeing   ❑ ....
❑ Canoeing   ❑ Skijoring   ❑ Swimming   ❑ ....

Facilities

❑ ADA   ❑ Visitor Center   ❑ Museum   ❑ ....
❑ Gift Shop   ❑ Picnic Sites   ❑ Restrooms   ❑ ....

Notes

....
....
....
....

Passport Stamps

Parker Dam State Park

Clearfield

DATE(S) VISITED:..

☐ SPRING   ☐ SUMMER   ☐ FALL   ☐ WINTER

WEATHER	TEMP:
☀ ☀☁ ☁ ☁ ☁ ☁	
☐ ☐ ☐ ☐ ☐ ☐	

Check In:.............................. Check Out:...............................

Lodging:.................................. Park hours:........................

Who I Went With:...

Fee(s):.. Will I Return?   YES / NO

Rating ★★★★★

Activities

☐ ATV/OHV	☐ Horseback Riding	☐ Fishing	☐ Wildlife
☐ Berry Picking	☐ Kayaking	☐ Hiking	☐ Bird Viewing
☐ Biking	☐ Photography	☐ Hunting	☐ Snowmobiling
☐ Boating	☐ Skiing	☐ Snowshoeing	☐ ....
☐ Canoeing	☐ Skijoring	☐ Swimming	☐ ....

Facilities

☐ ADA	☐ Visitor Center	☐ Museum	☐ ....
☐ Gift Shop	☐ Picnic Sites	☐ Restrooms	☐ ....

Notes
....
....
....
....

Passport Stamps

Patterson State Park

Potter

DATE(S) VISITED:..

❑ SPRING   ❑ SUMMER   ❑ FALL   ❑ WINTER

WEATHER					
❑	❑	❑	❑	❑	❑

TEMP:

Check In:................................ Check Out:...............................

Lodging:................................ Park hours:.........................

Who I Went With:...

Fee(s):.. Will I Return?   YES / NO

ABOUT THIS STATE PARK

Located in a remote area, Patterson has two rustic picnic pavilions for visitors to enjoy a quiet lunch. Patterson is a trailhead for the Susquehannock Trail, a favorite of backpackers.

Rating ★ ★ ★ ★ ★

Activities

- ❑ ATV/OHV
- ❑ Berry Picking
- ❑ Biking
- ❑ Boating
- ❑ Canoeing

- ❑ Horseback Riding
- ❑ Kayaking
- ❑ Photography
- ❑ Skiing
- ❑ Skijoring

- ❑ Fishing
- ❑ Hiking
- ❑ Hunting
- ❑ Snowshoeing
- ❑ Swimming

- ❑ Wildlife
- ❑ Bird Viewing
- ❑ Snowmobiling
- ❑ ....
- ❑ ....

Facilities

- ❑ ADA
- ❑ Gift Shop

- ❑ Visitor Center
- ❑ Picnic Sites

- ❑ Museum
- ❑ Restrooms

- ❑ ....
- ❑ ....

Notes

....
....
....
....

Passport Stamps

Penn-Roosevelt State Park

Centre

DATE(S) VISITED:..

☐ SPRING   ☐ SUMMER   ☐ FALL   ☐ WINTER

WEATHER	TEMP:
☀ ☐ ❄☁ ☐ ☁ ☐ 🌧 ☐ 🌧 ☐ 🌨 ☐	

Check In:............................ Check Out:...............................

Lodging:................................ Park hours:........................

Who I Went With:...

Fee(s):.. Will I Return?   YES / NO

Rating ★ ★ ★ ★ ★

Activities

☐ ATV/OHV
☐ Berry Picking
☐ Biking
☐ Boating
☐ Canoeing

☐ Horseback Riding
☐ Kayaking
☐ Photography
☐ Skiing
☐ Skijoring

☐ Fishing
☐ Hiking
☐ Hunting
☐ Snowshoeing
☐ Swimming

☐ Wildlife
☐ Bird Viewing
☐ Snowmobiling
☐ ....
☐ ....

Facilities

☐ ADA
☐ Gift Shop

☐ Visitor Center
☐ Picnic Sites

☐ Museum
☐ Restrooms

☐ ....
☐ ....

Notes

....
....
....
....

Passport Stamps

Pine Grove Furnace State Park   Cumberland

DATE(S) VISITED:..

❑ SPRING   ❑ SUMMER   ❑ FALL   ❑ WINTER

WEATHER		TEMP:

❑   ❑   ❑   ❑   ❑   ❑

Check In:............................. Check Out:.............................

Lodging:.................................. Park hours:........................

Who I Went With:...

Fee(s):... Will I Return?   YES / NO

Rating ★ ★ ★ ★ ★

Activities

❑ ATV/OHV   ❑ Horseback Riding   ❑ Fishing   ❑ Wildlife
❑ Berry Picking   ❑ Kayaking   ❑ Hiking   ❑ Bird Viewing
❑ Biking   ❑ Photography   ❑ Hunting   ❑ Snowmobiling
❑ Boating   ❑ Skiing   ❑ Snowshoeing   ❑ ....
❑ Canoeing   ❑ Skijoring   ❑ Swimming   ❑ ....

Facilities

❑ ADA   ❑ Visitor Center   ❑ Museum   ❑ ....
❑ Gift Shop   ❑ Picnic Sites   ❑ Restrooms   ❑ ....

Notes

....
....
....
....

Passport Stamps

Poe Paddy State Park

DATE(S) VISITED:..

❑ SPRING ❑ SUMMER ❑ FALL ❑ WINTER

WEATHER	TEMP:

❑ ❑ ❑ ❑ ❑ ❑

Check In:............................. Check Out:.............................

Lodging:.................................. Park hours:.......................

Who I Went With:...

Fee(s):.. Will I Return? YES / NO

Rating
★ ★ ★ ★ ★

ABOUT THIS STATE PARK

Poe Paddy State Park is at the confluence of Big Poe Creek and Penns Creek, a trout angler's paradise featuring the nationally recognized green drake mayfly hatch in June. Hikers enjoy the Mid State Trail. Poe Valley State Park is nearby.

Activities

❑ ATV/OHV   ❑ Horseback Riding   ❑ Fishing   ❑ Wildlife
❑ Berry Picking   ❑ Kayaking   ❑ Hiking   ❑ Bird Viewing
❑ Biking   ❑ Photography   ❑ Hunting   ❑ Snowmobiling
❑ Boating   ❑ Skiing   ❑ Snowshoeing   ❑ ....
❑ Canoeing   ❑ Skijoring   ❑ Swimming   ❑ ....

Facilities

❑ ADA   ❑ Visitor Center   ❑ Museum   ❑ ....
❑ Gift Shop   ❑ Picnic Sites   ❑ Restrooms ❑ ....

Notes
....
....
....
....

Passport Stamps

Poe Valley State Park

DATE(S) VISITED:..

❑ SPRING ❑ SUMMER ❑ FALL ❑ WINTER

WEATHER	TEMP:

☀ ❄☁ ☁ ☁ ☁ ☁
❑ ❑ ❑ ❑ ❑ ❑

Check In:............................ Check Out:............................

Lodging:................................. Park hours:........................

Who I Went With:..

Fee(s):... Will I Return? YES / NO

Rating
★ ★ ★ ★ ★

ABOUT THIS STATE PARK

Cozy Poe Valley State Park is nestled in a rugged mountain valley in Centre County. Seemingly endless forests surround the 25-acre Poe Lake. The 620-acre state park is surrounded by the 198,000-acre Bald Eagle State Forest.

Activities

❑ ATV/OHV	❑ Horseback Riding	❑ Fishing	❑ Wildlife
❑ Berry Picking	❑ Kayaking	❑ Hiking	❑ Bird Viewing
❑ Biking	❑ Photography	❑ Hunting	❑ Snowmobiling
❑ Boating	❑ Skiing	❑ Snowshoeing	❑ ....
❑ Canoeing	❑ Skijoring	❑ Swimming	❑ ....

Facilities

❑ ADA	❑ Visitor Center	❑ Museum	❑ ....
❑ Gift Shop	❑ Picnic Sites	❑ Restrooms	❑ ....

Notes
....
....
....
....

Passport Stamps

Point State Park

DATE(S) VISITED:...

❑ SPRING   ❑ SUMMER   ❑ FALL   ❑ WINTER

WEATHER	TEMP:
☀ ❄☁ ☁ ☁🌧 ☁🌧 ☁🌨	
❑ ❑ ❑ ❑ ❑ ❑	

ABOUT THIS STATE PARK

Point State Park, located at the confluence of three rivers, is at the tip of Pittsburgh's "Golden Triangle." The park commemorates and preserves the strategic and historic heritage of the area during the French and Indian War (1754-1763). Point State Park is a National Historic Landmark. DCNR works in collaboration with the Heinz History Center and the Fort Pitt Society of the Daughters of the American Revolution to interpret the history of the Forks of the Ohio.

Check In:............................. Check Out:..............................

Lodging:.................................. Park hours:.......................

Who I Went With:...

Fee(s):... Will I Return?   YES / NO

Rating ★ ★ ★ ★ ★

Activities

❑ ATV/OHV   ❑ Horseback Riding   ❑ Fishing   ❑ Wildlife
❑ Berry Picking   ❑ Kayaking   ❑ Hiking   ❑ Bird Viewing
❑ Biking   ❑ Photography   ❑ Hunting   ❑ Snowmobiling
❑ Boating   ❑ Skiing   ❑ Snowshoeing   ❑ ....
❑ Canoeing   ❑ Skijoring   ❑ Swimming   ❑ ....

Facilities

❑ ADA   ❑ Visitor Center   ❑ Museum   ❑ ....
❑ Gift Shop   ❑ Picnic Sites   ❑ Restrooms   ❑ ....

Notes

....
....
....
....

Passport Stamps

Presque Isle State Park

DATE(S) VISITED:..

❑ SPRING ❑ SUMMER ❑ FALL ❑ WINTER

WEATHER			TEMP:		
☀ ❑	⛅ ❑	☁ ❑	🌧 ❑	🌨 ❑	🌦 ❑

ABOUT THIS STATE PARK

Presque Isle State Park is a 3,200-acre sandy peninsula that arches into Lake Erie. As Pennsylvania's only "seashore," Presque Isle offers its visitors a beautiful coastline and many recreational activities, including swimming, boating, fishing, hiking, bicycling, and in-line skating. Presque Isle is a day-use park that provides year-round recreational opportunities. Overnight accommodations are available nearby.

Check In:............................. Check Out:..............................

Lodging:................................. Park hours:........................

Who I Went With:...

Fee(s):................................... Will I Return? YES / NO

Rating ★ ★ ★ ★ ★

Activities

❑ ATV/OHV	❑ Horseback Riding	❑ Fishing	❑ Wildlife
❑ Berry Picking	❑ Kayaking	❑ Hiking	❑ Bird Viewing
❑ Biking	❑ Photography	❑ Hunting	❑ Snowmobiling
❑ Boating	❑ Skiing	❑ Snowshoeing	❑ ....
❑ Canoeing	❑ Skijoring	❑ Swimming	❑ ....

Facilities

❑ ADA	❑ Visitor Center	❑ Museum	❑ ....
❑ Gift Shop	❑ Picnic Sites	❑ Restrooms	❑ ....

Notes
....
....
....
....

Passport Stamps

Prince Gallitzin State Park

Cambria

DATE(S) VISITED:...

❑ SPRING   ❑ SUMMER   ❑ FALL   ❑ WINTER

WEATHER	TEMP:
☀ ❑ ❄☁ ❑ ☁ ❑ ☔ ❑ 🌧 ❑ 🌨 ❑	

Check In:........................... Check Out:...............................

Lodging:................................ Park hours:........................

Who I Went With:...

Fee(s):............................ Will I Return? YES / NO

Rating ★ ★ ★ ★ ★

ABOUT THIS STATE PARK

At Prince Gallitzin State Park, the forested hills of the Allegheny Plateau cradle sprawling Glendale Lake. Vistas offer scenic views of the 1,635-acre lake with its 26 miles of shoreline, which is a favorite of anglers and boaters. Campers flock to the large campground and also enjoy hiking and other outdoor activities. The varied habitats of the park make it a home for many types of wildlife, and a rest stop in the spring and fall migrations.

Activities

❑ ATV/OHV	❑ Horseback Riding	❑ Fishing	❑ Wildlife
❑ Berry Picking	❑ Kayaking	❑ Hiking	❑ Bird Viewing
❑ Biking	❑ Photography	❑ Hunting	❑ Snowmobiling
❑ Boating	❑ Skiing	❑ Snowshoeing	❑ ....
❑ Canoeing	❑ Skijoring	❑ Swimming	❑ ....

Facilities

❑ ADA	❑ Visitor Center	❑ Museum	❑ ....
❑ Gift Shop	❑ Picnic Sites	❑ Restrooms	❑ ....

Notes

....
....
....
....

Passport Stamps

Promised Land State Park

DATE(S) VISITED:..

❑ SPRING   ❑ SUMMER   ❑ FALL   ❑ WINTER

WEATHER	TEMP:

☀ ❑   ☁ ❑   ☁ ❑   🌧 ❑   🌦 ❑   🌨 ❑

Check In:............................ Check Out:...........................

Lodging:.................................. Park hours:.......................

Who I Went With:...

Fee(s):.. Will I Return?   YES / NO

Rating ★ ★ ★ ★ ★

ABOUT THIS STATE PARK

About 3,000 acres in size, Promised Land State Park is on the Pocono Plateau, 1,800 feet above sea level, and is surrounded by 12,464 acres of the Delaware State Forest, including natural areas. Visitors can enjoy: Fishing and boating in two lakes. Rustic cabins. Camping. Miles of hiking trails. Exploring the forests. The forests of the park consist primarily of beech, oak, maple, and hemlock trees. Two lakes and several small streams add to the park's outstanding scenic beauty.

Activities

❑ ATV/OHV	❑ Horseback Riding	❑ Fishing	❑ Wildlife
❑ Berry Picking	❑ Kayaking	❑ Hiking	❑ Bird Viewing
❑ Biking	❑ Photography	❑ Hunting	❑ Snowmobiling
❑ Boating	❑ Skiing	❑ Snowshoeing	❑ ....
❑ Canoeing	❑ Skijoring	❑ Swimming	❑ ....

Facilities

❑ ADA	❑ Visitor Center	❑ Museum	❑ ....
❑ Gift Shop	❑ Picnic Sites	❑ Restrooms	❑ ....

Notes

....
....
....
....

Passport Stamps

Prompton State Park

Wayne

DATE(S) VISITED:..

❑ SPRING ❑ SUMMER ❑ FALL ❑ WINTER

| WEATHER | | TEMP: |

☀ ❄☁ ☁ 🌧 🌦 🌨
❑ ❑ ❑ ❑ ❑ ❑

Check In:.............................. Check Out:...............................

Lodging:.................................. Park hours:........................

Who I Went With:..

Fee(s):.. Will I Return? YES / NO

Rating ⭐ ⭐ ⭐ ⭐ ⭐

ABOUT THIS STATE PARK

Prompton State Park provides boat launching and picnicking facilities to the 290-acre Prompton Lake, which is operated by the U.S. Army Corps of Engineers. Twenty-six miles of hiking trails surround the lake.

Activities

❑ ATV/OHV	❑ Horseback Riding	❑ Fishing	❑ Wildlife
❑ Berry Picking	❑ Kayaking	❑ Hiking	❑ Bird Viewing
❑ Biking	❑ Photography	❑ Hunting	❑ Snowmobiling
❑ Boating	❑ Skiing	❑ Snowshoeing	❑ ....
❑ Canoeing	❑ Skijoring	❑ Swimming	❑ ....

Facilities

❑ ADA	❑ Visitor Center	❑ Museum	❑ ....
❑ Gift Shop	❑ Picnic Sites	❑ Restrooms	❑ ....

Notes

....
....
....
....

Passport Stamps

Prouty Place State Park

Potter

DATE(S) VISITED:...

❏ SPRING   ❏ SUMMER   ❏ FALL   ❏ WINTER

WEATHER	TEMP:

☀ ❏   ❄☁ ❏   ☁ ❏   🌧 ❏   🌧 ❏   🌨 ❏

The five-acre Prouty Place State Park is five miles southwest of PA 44 along Long Toe Road. This remote park offers access to hunting, fishing, and hiking within the surrounding Susquehannock State Forest.

Check In:............................ Check Out:............................

Lodging:.............................. Park hours:.......................

Who I Went With:...

Fee(s):................................. Will I Return? YES / NO

Rating ⭐ ⭐ ⭐ ⭐ ⭐

Activities

❏ ATV/OHV	❏ Horseback Riding	❏ Fishing	❏ Wildlife
❏ Berry Picking	❏ Kayaking	❏ Hiking	❏ Bird Viewing
❏ Biking	❏ Photography	❏ Hunting	❏ Snowmobiling
❏ Boating	❏ Skiing	❏ Snowshoeing	❏ ....
❏ Canoeing	❏ Skijoring	❏ Swimming	❏ ....

Facilities

❏ ADA	❏ Visitor Center	❏ Museum	❏ ....
❏ Gift Shop	❏ Picnic Sites	❏ Restrooms	❏ ....

Notes

....
....
....
....

Passport Stamps

Pymatuning State Park

Crawford

DATE(S) VISITED:..

❑ SPRING   ❑ SUMMER   ❑ FALL   ❑ WINTER

WEATHER		TEMP:

☀ ❑   🌤 ❑   ☁ ❑   🌧 ❑   🌧 ❑   🌨 ❑

Check In:............................ Check Out:..............................

Lodging:.................................. Park hours:........................

Who I Went With:..

Fee(s):.. Will I Return? YES / NO

Rating ★ ★ ★ ★ ★

Activities

❑ ATV/OHV
❑ Berry Picking
❑ Biking
❑ Boating
❑ Canoeing

❑ Horseback Riding
❑ Kayaking
❑ Photography
❑ Skiing
❑ Skijoring

❑ Fishing
❑ Hiking
❑ Hunting
❑ Snowshoeing
❑ Swimming

❑ Wildlife
❑ Bird Viewing
❑ Snowmobiling
❑ ....
❑ ....

Facilities

❑ ADA
❑ Gift Shop

❑ Visitor Center
❑ Picnic Sites

❑ Museum
❑ Restrooms

❑ ....
❑ ....

Notes

....
....
....
....

Passport Stamps

Raccoon Creek State Park

DATE(S) VISITED:..

❏ SPRING ❏ SUMMER ❏ FALL ❏ WINTER

WEATHER	TEMP:

❏ ❏ ❏ ❏ ❏ ❏

Check In:............................. Check Out:.............................

Lodging:............................. Park hours:.........................

Who I Went With:...

Fee(s):.. Will I Return? YES / NO

Rating ★ ★ ★ ★ ★

ABOUT THIS STATE PARK

Raccoon Creek State Park is one of Pennsylvania's largest and most visited state parks. It began as a Recreational Demonstration Area operated by the National Park Service in the 1930s during the Civilian Conservation Corps (CCC) era. The park encompasses 7,572 acres and features the beautiful 101-acre Raccoon Lake. Facilities are a mix of modern and rustic with group camps from the CCC era.

Activities

❏ ATV/OHV	❏ Horseback Riding	❏ Fishing	❏ Wildlife
❏ Berry Picking	❏ Kayaking	❏ Hiking	❏ Bird Viewing
❏ Biking	❏ Photography	❏ Hunting	❏ Snowmobiling
❏ Boating	❏ Skiing	❏ Snowshoeing	❏ ....
❏ Canoeing	❏ Skijoring	❏ Swimming	❏ ....

Facilities

❏ ADA	❏ Visitor Center	❏ Museum	❏ ....
❏ Gift Shop	❏ Picnic Sites	❏ Restrooms	❏ ....

Notes

....
....
....
....

Passport Stamps

Ralph Stover State Park

DATE(S) VISITED:...

☐ SPRING   ☐ SUMMER   ☐ FALL   ☐ WINTER

WEATHER	TEMP:
☀ ☀☁ ☁ 🌧 🌧 🌨	
☐ ☐ ☐ ☐ ☐ ☐	

Check In:............................. Check Out:.............................

Lodging:................................ Park hours:.......................

Who I Went With:...

Fee(s):................................. Will I Return?   YES / NO

Rating ⭐ ⭐ ⭐ ⭐ ⭐

ABOUT THIS STATE PARK

Tohickon Creek flows through the 45-acre Ralph Stover State Park, making a scenic picnic area. The nearby High Rocks section of the park is a lovely overlook of the Tohickon Creek.

Activities

☐ ATV/OHV	☐ Horseback Riding	☐ Fishing	☐ Wildlife
☐ Berry Picking	☐ Kayaking	☐ Hiking	☐ Bird Viewing
☐ Biking	☐ Photography	☐ Hunting	☐ Snowmobiling
☐ Boating	☐ Skiing	☐ Snowshoeing	☐ ....
☐ Canoeing	☐ Skijoring	☐ Swimming	☐ ....

Facilities

☐ ADA	☐ Visitor Center	☐ Museum	☐ ....
☐ Gift Shop	☐ Picnic Sites	☐ Restrooms	☐ ....

Notes

....
....
....
....

Passport Stamps

Ravensburg State Park

DATE(S) VISITED:..

❑ SPRING   ❑ SUMMER   ❑ FALL   ❑ WINTER

WEATHER			TEMP:		
☀	⛅	☁	🌧	🌦	🌨
❑	❑	❑	❑	❑	❑

Check In:............................ Check Out:............................

Lodging:................................. Park hours:........................

Who I Went With:...

Fee(s):.. Will I Return?   YES / NO

Rating   ★ ★ ★ ★ ★

ABOUT THIS STATE PARK

The park lies in a cozy, steep-walled gorge carved by Rauchtown Run through the side of Nippenose Mountain. A northern hardwood forest blankets the bottomland along this spring-fed stream. Talus (rock) covered slopes and interesting rock formations are interspersed among a stunted oak forest growing on the steep mountainsides and ridges. This pretty valley is especially beautiful when the mountain laurel blooms during late June and the fall foliage of early October.

Activities

❑ ATV/OHV	❑ Horseback Riding	❑ Fishing	❑ Wildlife
❑ Berry Picking	❑ Kayaking	❑ Hiking	❑ Bird Viewing
❑ Biking	❑ Photography	❑ Hunting	❑ Snowmobiling
❑ Boating	❑ Skiing	❑ Snowshoeing	❑ ....
❑ Canoeing	❑ Skijoring	❑ Swimming	❑ ....

Facilities

❑ ADA	❑ Visitor Center	❑ Museum	❑ ....
❑ Gift Shop	❑ Picnic Sites	❑ Restrooms	❑ ....

Notes

....
....
....
....

Passport Stamps

R. B. Winter State Park

Union

DATE(S) VISITED:..

❑ SPRING   ❑ SUMMER   ❑ FALL   ❑ WINTER

WEATHER	TEMP:
☀ ❑ 🌤 ❑ ☁ ❑ 🌧 ❑ 🌦 ❑ 🌨 ❑	

Check In:............................ Check Out:...............................

Lodging:.................................. Park hours:........................

Who I Went With:..

Fee(s):.. Will I Return?   YES / NO

Rating   ★ ★ ★ ★ ★

Activities

❑ ATV/OHV   ❑ Horseback Riding   ❑ Fishing   ❑ Wildlife
❑ Berry Picking   ❑ Kayaking   ❑ Hiking   ❑ Bird Viewing
❑ Biking   ❑ Photography   ❑ Hunting   ❑ Snowmobiling
❑ Boating   ❑ Skiing   ❑ Snowshoeing   ❑ ....
❑ Canoeing   ❑ Skijoring   ❑ Swimming   ❑ ....

Facilities

❑ ADA   ❑ Visitor Center   ❑ Museum   ❑ ....
❑ Gift Shop   ❑ Picnic Sites   ❑ Restrooms   ❑ ....

Notes

....
....
....
....

Passport Stamps

Reeds Gap State Park

DATE(S) VISITED:..

❑ SPRING   ❑ SUMMER   ❑ FALL   ❑ WINTER

WEATHER			TEMP:		
☀	❄☁	☁	☁🌧	☁🌧	☁🌨
❑	❑	❑	❑	❑	❑

ABOUT THIS STATE PARK

Reeds Gap State Park is 220 acres of wilderness in the New Lancaster Valley of Mifflin County. Large hemlocks and white pines cast cool shadows over Honey Creek, which flows through the park.

Check In:............................. Check Out:.............................

Lodging:................................. Park hours:........................

Who I Went With:...

Fee(s):................................. Will I Return?   YES / NO

Rating ⭐⭐⭐⭐⭐

Activities

❑ ATV/OHV	❑ Horseback Riding	❑ Fishing	❑ Wildlife
❑ Berry Picking	❑ Kayaking	❑ Hiking	❑ Bird Viewing
❑ Biking	❑ Photography	❑ Hunting	❑ Snowmobiling
❑ Boating	❑ Skiing	❑ Snowshoeing	❑ ....
❑ Canoeing	❑ Skijoring	❑ Swimming	❑ ....

Facilities

❑ ADA	❑ Visitor Center	❑ Museum	❑ ....
❑ Gift Shop	❑ Picnic Sites	❑ Restrooms	❑ ....

Notes

....
....
....
....

Passport Stamps

Ricketts Glen State Park

DATE(S) VISITED:..

❏ SPRING   ❏ SUMMER   ❏ FALL   ❏ WINTER

WEATHER	TEMP:

❏   ❏   ❏   ❏   ❏   ❏

Check In:............................ Check Out:............................

Lodging:............................ Park hours:........................

Who I Went With:...

Fee(s):.. Will I Return?   YES / NO

Rating ★ ★ ★ ★ ★

ABOUT THIS STATE PARK

Ricketts Glen State Park is one of the most scenic areas in Pennsylvania. This large park is comprised of 13,193 acres in Luzerne, Sullivan, and Columbia counties. Ricketts Glen harbors the Glens Natural Area -- a National Natural Landmark. Hike the Falls Trail System to explore the glens, which boasts a series of wild, free-flowing waterfalls, each cascading through rock-strewn clefts in this ancient hillside.

Activities

❏ ATV/OHV	❏ Horseback Riding	❏ Fishing	❏ Wildlife
❏ Berry Picking	❏ Kayaking	❏ Hiking	❏ Bird Viewing
❏ Biking	❏ Photography	❏ Hunting	❏ Snowmobiling
❏ Boating	❏ Skiing	❏ Snowshoeing	❏ ....
❏ Canoeing	❏ Skijoring	❏ Swimming	❏ ....

Facilities

❏ ADA	❏ Visitor Center	❏ Museum	❏ ....
❏ Gift Shop	❏ Picnic Sites	❏ Restrooms	❏ ....

Notes

....
....
....
....

Passport Stamps

Ridley Creek State Park

Delaware

DATE(S) VISITED:...

☐ SPRING ☐ SUMMER ☐ FALL ☐ WINTER

WEATHER			TEMP:		
☀	☁	☁	🌧	🌧	🌧
☐	☐	☐	☐	☐	☐

Check In:............................ Check Out:............................

Lodging:............................ Park hours:............................

Who I Went With:..

Fee(s):............................ Will I Return? YES / NO

Rating ⭐ ⭐ ⭐ ⭐ ⭐

ABOUT THIS STATE PARK

Ridley Creek State Park encompasses more than 2,606 acres of Delaware County woodlands and meadows. The gently rolling terrain of the park, bisected by Ridley Creek, is only 16 miles from center city Philadelphia and is an oasis of open space in a growing urban area.

Activities

- ☐ ATV/OHV
- ☐ Berry Picking
- ☐ Biking
- ☐ Boating
- ☐ Canoeing
- ☐ Horseback Riding
- ☐ Kayaking
- ☐ Photography
- ☐ Skiing
- ☐ Skijoring
- ☐ Fishing
- ☐ Hiking
- ☐ Hunting
- ☐ Snowshoeing
- ☐ Swimming
- ☐ Wildlife
- ☐ Bird Viewing
- ☐ Snowmobiling
- ☐ ....
- ☐ ....

Facilities

- ☐ ADA
- ☐ Gift Shop
- ☐ Visitor Center
- ☐ Picnic Sites
- ☐ Museum
- ☐ Restrooms
- ☐ ....
- ☐ ....

Notes

....
....
....
....

Passport Stamps

Ryerson Station State Park

Greene

DATE(S) VISITED:..

☐ SPRING   ☐ SUMMER   ☐ FALL   ☐ WINTER

WEATHER	TEMP:

☀ ☐   ❄☁ ☐   ☁ ☐   ☁ 🌧 ☐   ☁ 🌧 ☐   ☁ ❄ ☐

ABOUT THIS STATE PARK

Ryerson Station State Park is in Greene County in the southwestern corner of Pennsylvania, near the West Virginia border. The 1,164-acre park features a swimming pool, campground, hiking, fishing, picnicking, and winter activities.

Check In:............................ Check Out:.............................

Lodging:................................. Park hours:......................

Who I Went With:...

Fee(s):... Will I Return?   YES / NO

Rating ★ ★ ★ ★ ★

Activities

☐ ATV/OHV	☐ Horseback Riding	☐ Fishing	☐ Wildlife
☐ Berry Picking	☐ Kayaking	☐ Hiking	☐ Bird Viewing
☐ Biking	☐ Photography	☐ Hunting	☐ Snowmobiling
☐ Boating	☐ Skiing	☐ Snowshoeing	☐ ....
☐ Canoeing	☐ Skijoring	☐ Swimming	☐ ....

Facilities

☐ ADA	☐ Visitor Center	☐ Museum	☐ ....
☐ Gift Shop	☐ Picnic Sites	☐ Restrooms	☐ ....

Notes

....
....
....
....

Passport Stamps

Salt Springs State Park

DATE(S) VISITED:..

❏ SPRING ❏ SUMMER ❏ FALL ❏ WINTER

| WEATHER | | TEMP: |

❏ ❏ ❏ ❏ ❏ ❏

Check In:............................. Check Out:...........................

Lodging:.................................. Park hours:.......................

Who I Went With:..

Fee(s):.. Will I Return? YES / NO

Rating ★ ★ ★ ★ ★

ABOUT THIS STATE PARK

The 405-acre Salt Springs State Park is in northeastern Pennsylvania, seven miles north of Montrose in Susquehanna County. Focal points of the park are the towering old growth hemlock trees, many estimated to be more than 300 years old, and the rocky gorge cut by Fall Brook with its three waterfalls.

Activities

❏ ATV/OHV	❏ Horseback Riding	❏ Fishing	❏ Wildlife
❏ Berry Picking	❏ Kayaking	❏ Hiking	❏ Bird Viewing
❏ Biking	❏ Photography	❏ Hunting	❏ Snowmobiling
❏ Boating	❏ Skiing	❏ Snowshoeing	❏ ....
❏ Canoeing	❏ Skijoring	❏ Swimming	❏ ....

Facilities

❏ ADA	❏ Visitor Center	❏ Museum	❏ ....
❏ Gift Shop	❏ Picnic Sites	❏ Restrooms	❏ ....

Notes

....

....

....

....

Passport Stamps

Samuel S. Lewis State Park

York

DATE(S) VISITED:...

☐ SPRING   ☐ SUMMER   ☐ FALL   ☐ WINTER

WEATHER	TEMP:
☀ ☐ 🌤 ☐ ☁ ☐ 🌧 ☐ 🌧 ☐ 🌨 ☐	

Check In:............................. Check Out:...............................

Lodging:.................................. Park hours:........................

Who I Went With:..

Fee(s):... Will I Return? YES / NO

Rating

⭐ ⭐ ⭐ ⭐ ⭐

ABOUT THIS STATE PARK

This 85-acre state park is dominated by Mt. Pisgah, an 885-foot-high ridge that separates Kreutz Creek Valley to the north and East Prospect Valley to the south. The park landscape also consists of mowed grass fields on the northern and eastern park slopes, a pine plantation in the southern area, and mature woods in the western section.

Activities

☐ ATV/OHV	☐ Horseback Riding	☐ Fishing	☐ Wildlife
☐ Berry Picking	☐ Kayaking	☐ Hiking	☐ Bird Viewing
☐ Biking	☐ Photography	☐ Hunting	☐ Snowmobiling
☐ Boating	☐ Skiing	☐ Snowshoeing	☐ ....
☐ Canoeing	☐ Skijoring	☐ Swimming	☐ ....

Facilities

☐ ADA	☐ Visitor Center	☐ Museum	☐ ....
☐ Gift Shop	☐ Picnic Sites	☐ Restrooms	☐ ....

Notes

....
....
....
....

Passport Stamps

Sand Bridge State Park

Union

DATE(S) VISITED:...

❑ SPRING   ❑ SUMMER   ❑ FALL   ❑ WINTER

WEATHER	TEMP:

❑   ❑   ❑   ❑   ❑   ❑

Check In:............................. Check Out:.............................

Lodging:................................. Park hours:.......................

Who I Went With:..

Fee(s):.. Will I Return?   YES / NO

Rating ★ ★ ★ ★ ★

ABOUT THIS STATE PARK

Rapid Run's lovely murmur and the sounds of birds pervade this lovely picnic spot. Rustic picnic pavilions hug the side of Seven Notch Mountain, conveniently at the side of PA 192.

Activities

❑ ATV/OHV	❑ Horseback Riding	❑ Fishing	❑ Wildlife
❑ Berry Picking	❑ Kayaking	❑ Hiking	❑ Bird Viewing
❑ Biking	❑ Photography	❑ Hunting	❑ Snowmobiling
❑ Boating	❑ Skiing	❑ Snowshoeing	❑ ....
❑ Canoeing	❑ Skijoring	❑ Swimming	❑ ....

Facilities

❑ ADA	❑ Visitor Center	❑ Museum	❑ ....
❑ Gift Shop	❑ Picnic Sites	❑ Restrooms	❑ ....

Notes

....
....
....
....

Passport Stamps

Shawnee State Park

DATE(S) VISITED:...

❑ SPRING   ❑ SUMMER   ❑ FALL   ❑ WINTER

WEATHER			TEMP:		
☀	❆☁	☁	☁ |||||	☁ ⋰	☁ ⋰
❑	❑	❑	❑	❑	❑

Check In:............................. Check Out:...............................

Lodging:.................................. Park hours:........................

Who I Went With:..

Fee(s):.. Will I Return?   YES / NO

Rating ★ ★ ★ ★ ★

ABOUT THIS STATE PARK

Shawnee State Park is 3,983 acres of Pennsylvania's scenic Ridge and Valley Province. Ten miles west of the historic town of Bedford along US 30, Shawnee has modern recreational facilities that blend into the natural environment. A focal point of the park is the 451-acre Shawnee Lake.

Activities

❑ ATV/OHV	❑ Horseback Riding	❑ Fishing	❑ Wildlife
❑ Berry Picking	❑ Kayaking	❑ Hiking	❑ Bird Viewing
❑ Biking	❑ Photography	❑ Hunting	❑ Snowmobiling
❑ Boating	❑ Skiing	❑ Snowshoeing	❑ ....
❑ Canoeing	❑ Skijoring	❑ Swimming	❑ ....

Facilities

❑ ADA	❑ Visitor Center	❑ Museum	❑ ....
❑ Gift Shop	❑ Picnic Sites	❑ Restrooms	❑ ....

Notes

....
....
....
....

Passport Stamps

Shikellamy State Park

DATE(S) VISITED:..

❏ SPRING ❏ SUMMER ❏ FALL ❏ WINTER

| WEATHER | | TEMP: |

❏ ❏ ❏ ❏ ❏ ❏

Check In:.............................. Check Out:...............................

Lodging:.................................... Park hours:........................

Who I Went With:...

Fee(s):.. Will I Return? YES / NO

Rating ★ ★ ★ ★ ★

ABOUT THIS STATE PARK

Shikellamy State Park is in Union and Northumberland counties. The 54-acre Shikellamy Marina is on the southern tip of Packers Island at the confluence of the West Branch and North Branch Susquehanna River, and offers hiking and biking trails, a marina, and boat launch.

The 78-acre Shikellamy Overlook is on the western shore of the Susquehanna River. A 360-foot cliff overlooks the confluence of the branches of the Susquehanna River.

Activities

❏ ATV/OHV
❏ Berry Picking
❏ Biking
❏ Boating
❏ Canoeing

❏ Horseback Riding
❏ Kayaking
❏ Photography
❏ Skiing
❏ Skijoring

❏ Fishing
❏ Hiking
❏ Hunting
❏ Snowshoeing
❏ Swimming

❏ Wildlife
❏ Bird Viewing
❏ Snowmobiling
❏ ....
❏ ....

Facilities

❏ ADA
❏ Gift Shop

❏ Visitor Center
❏ Picnic Sites

❏ Museum
❏ Restrooms

❏ ....
❏ ....

Notes

....
....
....
....

Passport Stamps

Simon B. Elliott State Park

Clearfield

DATE(S) VISITED:..

☐ SPRING ☐ SUMMER ☐ FALL ☐ WINTER

WEATHER	TEMP:

☐ ☐ ☐ ☐ ☐ ☐

Check In:................................ Check Out:...............................

Lodging:................................ Park hours:........................

Who I Went With:..

Fee(s):................................ Will I Return? YES / NO

Rating ★ ★ ★ ★ ★

Activities

☐ ATV/OHV
☐ Berry Picking
☐ Biking
☐ Boating
☐ Canoeing

☐ Horseback Riding
☐ Kayaking
☐ Photography
☐ Skiing
☐ Skijoring

☐ Fishing
☐ Hiking
☐ Hunting
☐ Snowshoeing
☐ Swimming

☐ Wildlife
☐ Bird Viewing
☐ Snowmobiling
☐ ....
☐ ....

Facilities

☐ ADA
☐ Gift Shop

☐ Visitor Center
☐ Picnic Sites

☐ Museum
☐ Restrooms

☐ ....
☐ ....

Notes

....
....
....
....

Passport Stamps

Sinnemahoning State Park

DATE(S) VISITED:...

❏ SPRING ❏ SUMMER ❏ FALL ❏ WINTER

| WEATHER | | TEMP: | |

❏ ❏ ❏ ❏ ❏ ❏

Check In:............................. Check Out:.............................

Lodging:.................................. Park hours:........................

Who I Went With:...

Fee(s):.. Will I Return? YES / NO

Rating ★ ★ ★ ★ ★

ABOUT THIS STATE PARK

Sinnemahoning State Park, located near the center of the Pennsylvania Wilds' scenic steep valleys region, encompasses 1,910 acres of beautiful scenery and outstanding wildlife habitat. The park is long and narrow and includes lands on both sides of First Fork Sinnemahoning Creek -- a major tributary to the Sinnemahoning Creek. At the southern end of the park, a 145-acre reservoir created by the George B. Stevenson dam provides excellent fishing and water recreation opportunities..

Activities

❏ ATV/OHV	❏ Horseback Riding	❏ Fishing	❏ Wildlife
❏ Berry Picking	❏ Kayaking	❏ Hiking	❏ Bird Viewing
❏ Biking	❏ Photography	❏ Hunting	❏ Snowmobiling
❏ Boating	❏ Skiing	❏ Snowshoeing	❏ ....
❏ Canoeing	❏ Skijoring	❏ Swimming	❏ ....

Facilities

❏ ADA	❏ Visitor Center	❏ Museum	❏ ....
❏ Gift Shop	❏ Picnic Sites	❏ Restrooms	❏ ....

Notes

....
....
....
....

Passport Stamps

Sizerville State Park

DATE(S) VISITED:..

❑ SPRING   ❑ SUMMER   ❑ FALL   ❑ WINTER

WEATHER	TEMP:
☀ ❄☁ ☁ ☁🌧 ☁🌧 ☁❄	
❑ ❑ ❑ ❑ ❑ ❑	

Check In:............................. Check Out:..............................

Lodging:.................................. Park hours:........................

Who I Went With:..

Fee(s):.. Will I Return?   YES / NO

Rating ⭐⭐⭐⭐⭐

ABOUT THIS STATE PARK

The 386-acre Sizerville State Park is nearly surrounded by Elk State Forest and is close to one of the largest blocks of state forest land in the commonwealth. Sizerville has many recreational and natural opportunities and is a good base for exploring nearby public lands.

Activities

❑ ATV/OHV	❑ Horseback Riding	❑ Fishing	❑ Wildlife
❑ Berry Picking	❑ Kayaking	❑ Hiking	❑ Bird Viewing
❑ Biking	❑ Photography	❑ Hunting	❑ Snowmobiling
❑ Boating	❑ Skiing	❑ Snowshoeing	❑ ....
❑ Canoeing	❑ Skijoring	❑ Swimming	❑ ....

Facilities

❑ ADA	❑ Visitor Center	❑ Museum	❑ ....
❑ Gift Shop	❑ Picnic Sites	❑ Restrooms	❑ ....

Notes

....
....
....
....

Passport Stamps

Susquehanna State Park

Lycoming

DATE(S) VISITED:..

❏ SPRING ❏ SUMMER ❏ FALL ❏ WINTER

WEATHER		TEMP:

☀ ❄☁ ☁ 🌧 🌧 🌨
❏ ❏ ❏ ❏ ❏ ❏

Check In:............................ Check Out:............................

Lodging:................................. Park hours:.......................

Who I Went With:..

Fee(s):.. Will I Return? YES / NO

Rating ⭐ ⭐ ⭐ ⭐ ⭐

Activities

❏ ATV/OHV   ❏ Horseback Riding   ❏ Fishing   ❏ Wildlife
❏ Berry Picking ❏ Kayaking   ❏ Hiking   ❏ Bird Viewing
❏ Biking   ❏ Photography   ❏ Hunting   ❏ Snowmobiling
❏ Boating   ❏ Skiing   ❏ Snowshoeing ❏ ....
❏ Canoeing   ❏ Skijoring   ❏ Swimming   ❏ ....

Facilities

❏ ADA   ❏ Visitor Center   ❏ Museum   ❏ ....
❏ Gift Shop ❏ Picnic Sites   ❏ Restrooms   ❏ ....

Notes

....
....
....
....

Passport Stamps

Susquehannock State Park
Lancaster

DATE(S) VISITED:..

❑ SPRING ❑ SUMMER ❑ FALL ❑ WINTER

WEATHER	TEMP:
☀ ❄☁ ☁ 🌧 🌦 🌨	
❑ ❑ ❑ ❑ ❑ ❑	

Check In:............................ Check Out:...............................

Lodging:................................. Park hours:........................

Who I Went With:..

Fee(s):.. Will I Return? YES / NO

Rating ⭐⭐⭐⭐⭐

Activities

❑ ATV/OHV
❑ Berry Picking
❑ Biking
❑ Boating
❑ Canoeing

❑ Horseback Riding
❑ Kayaking
❑ Photography
❑ Skiing
❑ Skijoring

❑ Fishing
❑ Hiking
❑ Hunting
❑ Snowshoeing
❑ Swimming

❑ Wildlife
❑ Bird Viewing
❑ Snowmobiling
❑ ....
❑ ....

Facilities

❑ ADA
❑ Gift Shop

❑ Visitor Center
❑ Picnic Sites

❑ Museum
❑ Restrooms

❑ ....
❑ ....

Notes

....
....
....
....

Passport Stamps

Swatara State Park

DATE(S) VISITED:....................

❑ SPRING ❑ SUMMER ❑ FALL ❑ WINTER

WEATHER		TEMP:			
☀	❄☁	☁	☁	☁	☁
❑	❑	❑	❑	❑	❑

Check In:............................ Check Out:............................

Lodging:............................ Park hours:............................

Who I Went With:............................

Fee(s):............................ Will I Return? YES / NO

Rating ⭐⭐⭐⭐⭐

ABOUT THIS STATE PARK

The 3,520-acre Swatara State Park consists of rolling fields and woodlands situated in the Swatara Valley, between Second and Blue mountains. The scenic Swatara Creek meanders the length of the park and is surrounded by forests and wetlands that support a diversity of wildlife.

Activities

❑ ATV/OHV	❑ Horseback Riding	❑ Fishing	❑ Wildlife
❑ Berry Picking	❑ Kayaking	❑ Hiking	❑ Bird Viewing
❑ Biking	❑ Photography	❑ Hunting	❑ Snowmobiling
❑ Boating	❑ Skiing	❑ Snowshoeing	❑ ....
❑ Canoeing	❑ Skijoring	❑ Swimming	❑ ....

Facilities

❑ ADA	❑ Visitor Center	❑ Museum	❑ ....
❑ Gift Shop	❑ Picnic Sites	❑ Restrooms	❑ ....

Notes

....

....

....

....

Passport Stamps

Tobyhanna State Park

Monroe and Wayne

DATE(S) VISITED:..

❏ SPRING   ❏ SUMMER   ❏ FALL   ❏ WINTER

WEATHER	TEMP:

☀ ❄☁ ☁ ☁ ☁ ☁
❏ ❏ ❏ ❏ ❏ ❏

Check In:............................ Check Out:...............................

Lodging:.................................. Park hours:........................

Who I Went With:...

Fee(s):.. Will I Return?   YES / NO

Rating ⭐ ⭐ ⭐ ⭐ ⭐

Activities

❏ ATV/OHV	❏ Horseback Riding	❏ Fishing	❏ Wildlife
❏ Berry Picking	❏ Kayaking	❏ Hiking	❏ Bird Viewing
❏ Biking	❏ Photography	❏ Hunting	❏ Snowmobiling
❏ Boating	❏ Skiing	❏ Snowshoeing	❏ ....
❏ Canoeing	❏ Skijoring	❏ Swimming	❏ ....

Facilities

❏ ADA	❏ Visitor Center	❏ Museum	❏ ....
❏ Gift Shop	❏ Picnic Sites	❏ Restrooms	❏ ....

Notes

....
....
....
....

Passport Stamps

Trough Creek State Park

DATE(S) VISITED:..

❑ SPRING   ❑ SUMMER   ❑ FALL   ❑ WINTER

WEATHER					TEMP:
❑	❑	❑	❑	❑	❑

Check In:............................. Check Out:.............................

Lodging:.................................. Park hours:......................

Who I Went With:...

Fee(s):....................................... Will I Return?   YES / NO

Rating   ★ ★ ★ ★ ★

ABOUT THIS STATE PARK

The 541-acre Trough Creek State Park is a scenic gorge formed as Great Trough Creek cuts through Terrace Mountain before emptying into Raystown Lake. Rugged hiking trails lead to wonders like Balanced Rock and Rainbow Falls. Rothrock State Forest and Raystown LakeOpens In A New Window border the park, making a large, contiguous area of public land for recreation.

Activities

❑ ATV/OHV	❑ Horseback Riding	❑ Fishing	❑ Wildlife
❑ Berry Picking	❑ Kayaking	❑ Hiking	❑ Bird Viewing
❑ Biking	❑ Photography	❑ Hunting	❑ Snowmobiling
❑ Boating	❑ Skiing	❑ Snowshoeing	❑ ....
❑ Canoeing	❑ Skijoring	❑ Swimming	❑ ....

Facilities

❑ ADA	❑ Visitor Center	❑ Museum	❑ ....
❑ Gift Shop	❑ Picnic Sites	❑ Restrooms	❑ ....

Notes

....
....
....
....

Passport Stamps

Tuscarora State Park

DATE(S) VISITED:..

❑ SPRING   ❑ SUMMER   ❑ FALL   ❑ WINTER

WEATHER	TEMP:
☀ ❑ ☀☁ ❑ ☁ ❑ ☁‖‖‖ ❑ ☁☔ ❑ ☁❄ ❑	

Check In:............................ Check Out:...............................

Lodging:.................................. Park hours:........................

Who I Went With:..

Fee(s):.. Will I Return?   YES / NO

Rating ★ ★ ★ ★ ★

Activities

❑ ATV/OHV	❑ Horseback Riding	❑ Fishing	❑ Wildlife
❑ Berry Picking	❑ Kayaking	❑ Hiking	❑ Bird Viewing
❑ Biking	❑ Photography	❑ Hunting	❑ Snowmobiling
❑ Boating	❑ Skiing	❑ Snowshoeing	❑ ....
❑ Canoeing	❑ Skijoring	❑ Swimming	❑ ....

Facilities

❑ ADA	❑ Visitor Center	❑ Museum	❑ ....
❑ Gift Shop	❑ Picnic Sites	❑ Restrooms	❑ ....

Notes

....
....
....
....

Passport Stamps

Tyler State Park

DATE(S) VISITED:..

❑ SPRING   ❑ SUMMER   ❑ FALL   ❑ WINTER

WEATHER				TEMP:	
☀	☁	☁	☁	☁	☁
❑	❑	❑	❑	❑	❑

Check In:................................ Check Out:.............................

Lodging:.................................. Park hours:.......................

Who I Went With:...

Fee(s):... Will I Return?   YES / NO

Rating ⭐ ⭐ ⭐ ⭐ ⭐

ABOUT THIS STATE PARK

Located 33 miles from Center City Philadelphia, Tyler State Park consists of 1,711 acres in Bucks County. Park roads, trails, and facilities are carefully nestled within the original farm and woodland setting. Neshaminy Creek meanders through the park, dividing the land into several interesting sections.

Activities

❑ ATV/OHV	❑ Horseback Riding	❑ Fishing	❑ Wildlife
❑ Berry Picking	❑ Kayaking	❑ Hiking	❑ Bird Viewing
❑ Biking	❑ Photography	❑ Hunting	❑ Snowmobiling
❑ Boating	❑ Skiing	❑ Snowshoeing	❑ ....
❑ Canoeing	❑ Skijoring	❑ Swimming	❑ ....

Facilities

❑ ADA	❑ Visitor Center	❑ Museum	❑ ....
❑ Gift Shop	❑ Picnic Sites	❑ Restrooms	❑ ....

Notes

....
....
....
....

Passport Stamps

Tyler State Park

DATE(S) VISITED:..

❑ SPRING   ❑ SUMMER   ❑ FALL   ❑ WINTER

WEATHER		TEMP:			
☀ ❑	🌤 ❑	☁ ❑	🌧 ❑	🌧 ❑	🌨 ❑

ABOUT THIS STATE PARK

Located 33 miles from Center City Philadelphia, Tyler State Park consists of 1,711 acres in Bucks County. Park roads, trails, and facilities are carefully nestled within the original farm and woodland setting. Neshaminy Creek meanders through the park, dividing the land into several interesting sections.

Check In:............................ Check Out:............................

Lodging:............................ Park hours:......................

Who I Went With:...

Fee(s):.. Will I Return?   YES / NO

Rating ⭐ ⭐ ⭐ ⭐ ⭐

Activities

❑ ATV/OHV   ❑ Horseback Riding   ❑ Fishing   ❑ Wildlife
❑ Berry Picking   ❑ Kayaking   ❑ Hiking   ❑ Bird Viewing
❑ Biking   ❑ Photography   ❑ Hunting   ❑ Snowmobiling
❑ Boating   ❑ Skiing   ❑ Snowshoeing   ❑ ....
❑ Canoeing   ❑ Skijoring   ❑ Swimming   ❑ ....

Facilities

❑ ADA   ❑ Visitor Center   ❑ Museum   ❑ ....
❑ Gift Shop   ❑ Picnic Sites   ❑ Restrooms   ❑ ....

Notes

....
....
....
....

Passport Stamps

Upper Pine Bottom State Park

Lycoming

DATE(S) VISITED:...

❏ SPRING   ❏ SUMMER   ❏ FALL   ❏ WINTER

WEATHER						TEMP:
☀ ❏	☁ ❏	☁ ❏	🌧 ❏	🌧 ❏	🌨 ❏	

Check In:.............................. Check Out:...........................

Lodging:................................. Park hours:........................

Who I Went With:...

Fee(s):... Will I Return?   YES / NO

Rating ★ ★ ★ ★ ★

Activities

❏ ATV/OHV	❏ Horseback Riding	❏ Fishing	❏ Wildlife
❏ Berry Picking	❏ Kayaking	❏ Hiking	❏ Bird Viewing
❏ Biking	❏ Photography	❏ Hunting	❏ Snowmobiling
❏ Boating	❏ Skiing	❏ Snowshoeing	❏ ....
❏ Canoeing	❏ Skijoring	❏ Swimming	❏ ....

Facilities

❏ ADA	❏ Visitor Center	❏ Museum	❏ ....
❏ Gift Shop	❏ Picnic Sites	❏ Restrooms	❏ ....

Notes

....
....
....
....

Passport Stamps

Varden Conservation Area

Wayne

DATE(S) VISITED:...

❑ SPRING   ❑ SUMMER   ❑ FALL   ❑ WINTER

WEATHER	TEMP:

☀   🌤   ☁   🌧   🌦   🌨
❑   ❑   ❑   ❑   ❑   ❑

Check In:............................. Check Out:.............................

Lodging:.................................. Park hours:........................

Who I Went With:..

Fee(s):.. Will I Return?   YES / NO

Rating   ⭐ ⭐ ⭐ ⭐ ⭐

ABOUT THIS STATE PARK

A gift from veterinarian Dr. Mead Shaffer, the 444-acre Varden Conservation Area is in Wayne County. This magnanimous gift is in an area that was once a remote section of the state, which is now beginning to feel the pressure of development. The land will be protected and used for future generations as a respite from daily life. Varden is a place to learn about Pennsylvania's wonderful natural history. The property is managed by Promised Land State Park.

Activities

❑ ATV/OHV	❑ Horseback Riding	❑ Fishing	❑ Wildlife
❑ Berry Picking	❑ Kayaking	❑ Hiking	❑ Bird Viewing
❑ Biking	❑ Photography	❑ Hunting	❑ Snowmobiling
❑ Boating	❑ Skiing	❑ Snowshoeing	❑ ....
❑ Canoeing	❑ Skijoring	❑ Swimming	❑ ....

Facilities

❑ ADA	❑ Visitor Center	❑ Museum	❑ ....
❑ Gift Shop	❑ Picnic Sites	❑ Restrooms	❑ ....

Notes

....
....
....
....

Passport Stamps

Warriors Path State Park

DATE(S) VISITED:..

❑ SPRING   ❑ SUMMER   ❑ FALL   ❑ WINTER

WEATHER			TEMP:		
☀ ❑	☁ ❑	☁ ❑	☁ ❑	☁ ❑	☁ ❑

ABOUT THIS STATE PARK

The 349-acre Warriors Path State Park lies very near the famous path used by the Iroquois in raids and wars with the Cherokees and other American Indians in southern Pennsylvania. The park is a seasonal, day-use area open from mid-April through the end of October. At other times of the year, visitors must park near the main gate and walk into the park.

Check In:............................. Check Out:.............................

Lodging:................................. Park hours:.......................

Who I Went With:...

Fee(s):................................. Will I Return?   YES / NO

Rating ★ ★ ★ ★ ★

Activities

❑ ATV/OHV	❑ Horseback Riding	❑ Fishing	❑ Wildlife
❑ Berry Picking	❑ Kayaking	❑ Hiking	❑ Bird Viewing
❑ Biking	❑ Photography	❑ Hunting	❑ Snowmobiling
❑ Boating	❑ Skiing	❑ Snowshoeing	❑ ....
❑ Canoeing	❑ Skijoring	❑ Swimming	❑ ....

Facilities

❑ ADA	❑ Visitor Center	❑ Museum	❑ ....
❑ Gift Shop	❑ Picnic Sites	❑ Restrooms	❑ ....

Notes

....
....
....
....

Passport Stamps

Washington Crossing Historic Park

Bucks

DATE(S) VISITED:..

❑ SPRING ❑ SUMMER ❑ FALL ❑ WINTER

WEATHER			TEMP:		
☀	☁	☁	☁	☁	☁
❑	❑	❑	❑	❑	❑

Check In:............................. Check Out:.............................

Lodging:.................................. Park hours:.......................

Who I Went With:...

Fee(s):... Will I Return? YES / NO

Rating ⭐ ⭐ ⭐ ⭐ ⭐

ABOUT THIS STATE PARK

Washington Crossing Historic Park preserves the site of George Washington's dramatic boat crossing of the Delaware River during the American Revolution and is a National Historic Landmark.
The Upper Section of the park has historic buildings, walking paths, picnic pavilions, fishing, and historical and environmental education programs. The Lower Section of the park has historic buildings, walking paths, picnicking, picnic pavilions, fishing, non-motorized boat launching, outdoor recreation programs.

Activities

❑ ATV/OHV	❑ Horseback Riding	❑ Fishing	❑ Wildlife
❑ Berry Picking	❑ Kayaking	❑ Hiking	❑ Bird Viewing
❑ Biking	❑ Photography	❑ Hunting	❑ Snowmobiling
❑ Boating	❑ Skiing	❑ Snowshoeing	❑ ....
❑ Canoeing	❑ Skijoring	❑ Swimming	❑ ....

Facilities

❑ ADA	❑ Visitor Center	❑ Museum	❑ ....
❑ Gift Shop	❑ Picnic Sites	❑ Restrooms	❑ ....

Notes

....
....
....
....

Passport Stamps

Whipple Dam State Park

Huntingdon

DATE(S) VISITED:...

❏ SPRING ❏ SUMMER ❏ FALL ❏ WINTER

WEATHER	TEMP:
☀ ❏ ☁❄ ❏ ☁ ❏ ☁ ❏ ☁ ❏ ☁ ❏	

Check In:............................ Check Out:............................

Lodging:................................. Park hours:.......................

Who I Went With:...

Fee(s):................................. Will I Return? YES / NO

Rating ★ ★ ★ ★ ★

ABOUT THIS STATE PARK

The 256-acre Whipple Dam State Park is a delightful and quiet place to visit. The lake is the perfect place to indulge in a refreshing dip, bird watch, or just relax. The beautiful day-use area is wonderful for a picnic or hike.

Activities

❏ ATV/OHV
❏ Berry Picking
❏ Biking
❏ Boating
❏ Canoeing

❏ Horseback Riding
❏ Kayaking
❏ Photography
❏ Skiing
❏ Skijoring

❏ Fishing
❏ Hiking
❏ Hunting
❏ Snowshoeing
❏ Swimming

❏ Wildlife
❏ Bird Viewing
❏ Snowmobiling
❏ ....
❏ ....

Facilities

❏ ADA
❏ Gift Shop

❏ Visitor Center
❏ Picnic Sites

❏ Museum
❏ Restrooms

❏ ....
❏ ....

Notes

....
....
....
....

Passport Stamps

White Clay Creek Preserve

Chester

DATE(S) VISITED:..

❏ SPRING ❏ SUMMER ❏ FALL ❏ WINTER

WEATHER	TEMP:
☀ ❏ ⛅ ❏ ☁ ❏ 🌧 ❏ 🌧 ❏ 🌦 ❏	

Check In:.............................. Check Out:..............................

Lodging:.................................. Park hours:.......................

Who I Went With:...

Fee(s):.. Will I Return? YES / NO

Rating ★ ★ ★ ★ ★

Activities

❏ ATV/OHV
❏ Berry Picking
❏ Biking
❏ Boating
❏ Canoeing

❏ Horseback Riding
❏ Kayaking
❏ Photography
❏ Skiing
❏ Skijoring

❏ Fishing
❏ Hiking
❏ Hunting
❏ Snowshoeing
❏ Swimming

❏ Wildlife
❏ Bird Viewing
❏ Snowmobiling
❏ ....
❏ ....

Facilities

❏ ADA
❏ Gift Shop

❏ Visitor Center
❏ Picnic Sites

❏ Museum
❏ Restrooms

❏ ....
❏ ....

Notes

....
....
....
....

Passport Stamps

Worlds End State Park

DATE(S) VISITED:...

❑ SPRING   ❑ SUMMER   ❑ FALL   ❑ WINTER

WEATHER	TEMP:
☀ ❑ ☁❄ ❑ ☁ ❑ ☁☂ ❑ ☁❄ ❑ ☁ ❑	

ABOUT THIS STATE PARK

Worlds End State Park is situated in a narrow S-shaped valley of the Loyalsock Creek, just south of Forksville, Sullivan County. Surrounded by the Loyalsock State Forest, the 780-acre park offers visitors diverse recreational opportunities within a pristine environment. The rugged natural beauty coursing through the heart of the Endless Mountains landscape provides many photographic possibilities.

Check In:.............................. Check Out:................................

Lodging:.................................. Park hours:........................

Who I Went With:..

Fee(s):... Will I Return?   YES / NO

Rating ★ ★ ★ ★ ★

Activities

❑ ATV/OHV   ❑ Horseback Riding   ❑ Fishing   ❑ Wildlife
❑ Berry Picking   ❑ Kayaking   ❑ Hiking   ❑ Bird Viewing
❑ Biking   ❑ Photography   ❑ Hunting   ❑ Snowmobiling
❑ Boating   ❑ Skiing   ❑ Snowshoeing   ❑ ....
❑ Canoeing   ❑ Skijoring   ❑ Swimming   ❑ ....

Facilities

❑ ADA   ❑ Visitor Center   ❑ Museum   ❑ ....
❑ Gift Shop   ❑ Picnic Sites   ❑ Restrooms   ❑ ....

Notes

....
....
....
....

Passport Stamps

Yellow Creek State Park

Indiana

DATE(S) VISITED:..

☐ SPRING ☐ SUMMER ☐ FALL ☐ WINTER

WEATHER	TEMP:

☀ ☐   🌤 ☐   ☁ ☐   🌧 ☐   🌧 ☐   🌨 ☐

Check In:............................. Check Out:.............................

Lodging:................................ Park hours:.......................

Who I Went With:...

Fee(s):... Will I Return?   YES / NO

Rating ★ ★ ★ ★ ★

Activities

☐ ATV/OHV   ☐ Horseback Riding   ☐ Fishing   ☐ Wildlife
☐ Berry Picking   ☐ Kayaking   ☐ Hiking   ☐ Bird Viewing
☐ Biking   ☐ Photography   ☐ Hunting   ☐ Snowmobiling
☐ Boating   ☐ Skiing   ☐ Snowshoeing   ☐ ....
☐ Canoeing   ☐ Skijoring   ☐ Swimming   ☐ ....

Facilities

☐ ADA   ☐ Visitor Center   ☐ Museum   ☐ ....
☐ Gift Shop ☐ Picnic Sites   ☐ Restrooms   ☐ ....

Notes

....
....
....
....

Passport Stamps

Made in the USA
Middletown, DE
07 August 2024